TEST BANK

Richard N. Aufmann
Palomar College

Vernon C. Barker
Palomar College

Joanne S. Lockwood
Plymouth State College

BASIC COLLEGE MATHEMATICS: AN APPLIED APPROACH

SEVENTH EDITION

Aufmann/Barker/Lockwood

HOUGHTON MIFFLIN COMPANY   BOSTON NEW YORK

Senior Sponsoring Editor: Lynn Cox
Senior Development Editor: Dawn Nuttall
Editorial Associate: Melissa Parkin
Senior Manufacturing Coordinator: Florence Cadran
Marketing Manager: Ben Rivera

Printed in the U.S.A.

ISBN: 0-618-20289-7

1 2 3 4 5 6 7 8 9- VHG -06 05 04 03 02

Test Bank

Chapter 1 Whole Numbers

Section 1.1 Introduction to Whole Numbers

Objective A: To identify the order relation between two numbers

Choose the correct symbol, >,<, or =.

1. 3434 ___ 2205

    (A) >   (B) <   (C) =

2. 316,987 ___ 298,187

    (A) >   (B) <   (C) =

3. 284,740 ___ 142,740

    (A) >   (B) <   (C) =

4. 11,229,581,082 ___ 11,229,582,902

    (A) >   (B) <   (C) =

5. Insert the correct symbol, >,<, or =, between the two numbers.
    300,269 ___ 353,089

Objective B: To write whole numbers in words and in standard form

6. Which shows four thousand, two hundred twenty-four in standard form?

    (A) 422   (B) 42,240   (C) 4224   (D) 4,000,224

7. Which shows two hundred thirty thousand, one hundred sixty-three in standard form?

    (A) 230,163   (B) 320,103   (C) 20,163   (D) 230,603

8. Which shows 2,991,357 in words?

    (A) two and nine hundred thousand, three hundred and fifty-seven

    (B) two million, nine hundred ninety thousand, three hundred fifty

    (C) two million, nine hundred ninety-one thousand, three hundred fifty-seven

    (D) nine thousand one, three hundred fifty-seven

9. Which shows 40,970,561 in words?

(A) forty million, nine hundred seventy thousand, five hundred sixty-one

(B) forty million, nine hundred sixty-eight thousand, two hundred, five hundred sixty-one

(C) forty million, nine hundred seventy thousand, four hundred fifty-one

(D) twenty-nine million, nine hundred seventy thousand, five hundred sixty-one

10. Write 504,856,907 in words.

Objective C: To write whole numbers in expanded form

11. Which shows 92814 in expanded form?

(A) $90,000 + 2000 + 100 + 40 + 8$

(B) $9000 + 200 + 10 + 4$

(C) $90,000 + 2000 + 800 + 10 + 4$

(D) $92,000 + 800 + 14$

12. Which shows 6,822,194 in expanded form?

(A) $6,000,000 + 800,000 + 20,000 + 2000 + 100 + 90 + 4$

(B) $800,000 + 200,000 + 20,000 + 1000 + 900 + 4$

(C) $6,000,000 + 800,000 + 20,000 + 2000 + 400 + 90 + 1$

(D) $600,000 + 80,000 + 200 + 2$

13. Which shows 39,439 in expanded form?

(A) $30,000 + 9 + 4 + 3 + 9$

(B) $30,000 + 9000 + 400 + 30 + 9$

(C) $39,000 + 400 + 30 + 9$

(D) $300,000 + 90,000 + 4000 + 30 + 9$

14. Which shows 772,649 in expanded form?

(A) $700,000 + 70,000 + 2000 + 600 + 40 + 9$

(B) $70,000 + 7000 + 200 + 60 + 9$

(C) $700,000 + 70,000 + 6000 + 200 + 90 + 4$

(D) $70,000 + 7000 + 600 + 49$

15. Write 63,713 in expanded form.

Objective D: To round a whole number to a given place value

16. Which shows 3363 rounded to the nearest hundred?

(A) 3300   (B) 3500   (C) 4000   (D) 3400

17. Which shows 34,654,433 rounded to the nearest ten thousand?

    (A) 34,640,000   (B) 34,660,000   (C) 34,700,000   (D) 34,650,000

18. Which shows 6642 rounded to the nearest thousand?

    (A) 7000   (B) 6600   (C) 5000   (D) 6000

19. Which shows 13,217,961 rounded to the nearest thousand?

    (A) 13,218,000   (B) 14,219,000   (C) 3,218,000   (D) 13,217,000

20. Round 41,325 to the nearest ten thousand.

Section 1.2: Addition of Whole Numbers

Objective A: To add whole numbers

Add.

21.   19,398
    +   1754

    (A) 21,252   (B) 21,142   (C) 21,152   (D) 21,147

22.   7,219,640
    + 5,298,665

    (A) 12,518,305   (B) 12,518,205   (C) 12,518,300   (D) 12,518,315

23. 462,437 + 334,039

    (A) 796,475   (B) 796,466   (C) 796,476   (D) 796,477

24. 68 + 152 + 3952

    (A) 4181   (B) 4189   (C) 4265   (D) 4172

25. 736,288 + 488,788

Objective B: To solve application problems

26. The parking strip is 427 feet long. The school board wants to extend it another 58 feet. How long would it then be?

    (A) 475 ft   (B) 485 ft   (C) 369 ft   (D) 585 ft

27. Josiah is a pilot for Sky High Airlines. His flight log showed that he traveled 5686 miles during the first week, 1416 miles during the second, and 4844 miles during the third week. How many miles did Josiah fly during this three week period?

    (A) 10,945   (B) 12,047   (C) 13,056   (D) 11,946

28. The following list shows the number of middle school students from three schools who signed up for outdoor school: Peterton, 137 students; Rutherford, 197 students; and Colton, 473 students. How many students signed up for outdoor school?

    (A) 826   (B) 807   (C) 717   (D) 854

29. Nutrition specialists often calculate calorie intake. The chart below shows calories for some common breakfast and luncheon foods. How many calories would a person consume if he or she had a lunch of a hot dog, french fries, and a glass of milk?

Food	Calories	Food	Calories
Banana	89	Cereal	115
Cola	80	Egg	81
French Fries	266	Hamburger	289
Hot Dog	131	Ice Cream	207
Milk (1 glass)	161	Milk Shake	275
Orange Juice	95	Toast	110

    (A) 558   (B) 407   (C) 568   (D) 397

30. The band club sold 4750 candy bars the first week of the fundraiser to buy new band uniforms. The second week 2016 candy bars were sold. How many candy bars were sold the first two weeks?

Section 1.3: Subtraction of Whole Numbers

Objective A: To subtract whole numbers without borrowing

Subtract.

31.   378
      − 45

(A) 333   (B) 327   (C) 313   (D) 343

32.   1376
      − 402

(A) 1678   (B) 874   (C) 1778   (D) 974

33. 8976 − 6255

(A) 2703   (B) 2721   (C) 15,231   (D) 2613

34. 632 − 402

(A) 1034   (B) 220   (C) 230   (D) 234

35. 626 − 402

Objective B: To subtract whole numbers with borrowing

Subtract.

36.   168
      − 99

(A) 59   (B) 75   (C) 69   (D) 79

37.   7901
      − 613

(A) 7188   (B) 8514   (C) 8414   (D) 7288

Subtract.

38.   5365
       − 2676

(A) 2679   (B) 2589   (C) 2688   (D) 2689

39. 775 − 367

(A) 528   (B) 422   (C) 1142   (D) 408

40.   7203
       − 432

Objective C: To solve application problems

41. Cameron worked 17 more hours this week than he did last week. If he worked 26 hours this week, how many hours did he work last week?

(A) 43   (B) 19   (C) 53   (D) 9

42. Carniola Mountain is 5483 feet in elevation. The top 1339 feet were in the sun. How many vertical feet of Carniola Mountain were in the shade?

(A) 4154   (B) 4244   (C) 4144   (D) 6822

43. The population of Texas in 1990 was 16,986,051 people. The population of Alabama was 4,040,587 people. How many more people lived in Texas?

(A) 12,937,464   (B) 12,945,444   (C) 12,945,464   (D) 12,475,464

44. The balance in a savings account is $8300. If $988 is withdrawn, how much money is left in the account?

(A) $7312   (B) $7317   (C) $7309   (D) $7315

45. The population of New York in 1990 was 17,990,455 people. The population of Montana was 799,065 people. How many more people lived in New York?

Section 1.4: To multiply a number by a single digit

Objective A: To multiply a number by a single digit

Multiply.

46.　94
$\times\ 7$

(A) 748　　　　(B) 658　　　　(C) 708　　　　(D) 618

47.　676
$\times\ 8$

(A) 5368　　　(B) 5408　　　(C) 5508　　　(D) 5468

48.　8538
$\times\ 4$

(A) 34,072　　(B) 35,212　　(C) 34,152　　(D) 33,932

49. 291×4

(A) 1264　　　(B) 1204　　　(C) 1154　　　(D) 1164

50. 260×5

Objective B: To multiply larger whole numbers

Multiply.

51.　301
$\times\ 48$

(A) 349　　　　(B) 144,480　　(C) 1444　　　(D) 14,448

52.　178
$\times\ 73$

(A) 13,994　　(B) 12,994　　(C) 13,094　　(D) 14,094

Multiply.

53.   138
      × 359

   (A) 49,442   (B) 48,542   (C) 49,532   (D) 49,542

54. 236 × 65

   (A) 16,340   (B) 15,440   (C) 15,340   (D) 16,440

55. 193 × 20

Objective C: To solve application problems

56. Tilda's Tours has 14 fifty-seven passenger buses in its fleet. How many people can Tilda's Tours take on all-day tours of Washington, D.C.?

   (A) 798   (B) 788   (C) 768   (D) 908

57. Mangledorn's Notions packs 169 buttons in each box. Pierce ordered 57 boxes of buttons. How many buttons did Pierce order?

   (A) 9633   (B) 9743   (C) 8613   (D) 8573

58. Betty will make loan payments of $320 each month for 24 months. What is the total amount of money that Betty will pay?

   (A) $7580   (B) $768   (C) $76,800   (D) $7680

59. George eats an average of 973 calories of food at each meal. How many calories will he eat in 10 meals?

   (A) 983   (B) 9830   (C) 97,300   (D) 9730

60. Tilda's Tours has 15 fifty-four passenger buses in its fleet. How many people can Tilda's Tours take on all-day tours of London?

Section 1.5: Division of Whole Numbers

Objective A: To divide by a single digit with no remainders in the quotient

Divide.

61. $2\overline{)222}$

(A) 108   (B) 102   (C) 112   (D) 111

62. $2\overline{)524}$

(A) 252   (B) 262   (C) 263   (D) 261

63. $9\overline{)756}$

(A) 83   (B) 92   (C) 74   (D) 84

64. $2\overline{)172}$

(A) 86   (B) 87   (C) 96   (D) 89

65. $2\overline{)984}$

Objective B: To divide by a single digit with a remainder in the quotient

Divide.

66. $4\overline{)802}$

(A) 203   (B) 200 r2   (C) 200 r4   (D) 199 r2

67. $5\overline{)219}$

(A) 42 r9   (B) 43 r4   (C) 42   (D) 47

68. $4\overline{)426}$

(A) 5 r1   (B) 6 r1   (C) 106 r2   (D) 105 r2

Divide.

69. 5)304

    (A) 60 r4   (B) 6 r4   (C) 64   (D) 64 r4

70. 4)313

Objective C: To divide by a larger whole number

Divide.

71. 55)17,875

    (A) 315   (B) 325   (C) 225   (D) 326

72. 67)15,477

    (A) 232   (B) 231   (C) 234   (D) 229

73. 723)383,190

    (A) 540   (B) 530   (C) 630   (D) 529

74. 622)47,921

    (A) 76 r38   (B) 78 r16   (C) 77 r27   (D) 93 r78

75. 502)33,668

Objective D: To solve application problems

76. Victor's annual salary of $25,200 is paid in 12 equal monthly payments. How much does Victor receive each month?

    (A) $2150   (B) $200   (C) $2000   (D) none of these

77. A charity receives $4,635,000 from 309 donors. If each donor gave an equal amount, how much did each donor give?

    (A) $16,000   (B) $15,000   (C) $24,000   (D) $25,000

78. Kurt's construction crew connected 49 drainage pipes to make a sewer line that was 343 feet long. How long was each pipe?

   (A) 7 ft   (B) 41 ft   (C) 294 ft   (D) 8 ft

79. Dan enjoys collecting baseball cards. His album contains 16 pages. If the album holds 192 cards, how many cards does each page hold?

   (A) 12   (B) 18   (C) 13   (D) 6

80. Gerda is asked to give an equal number of flower seeds to each of 27 classmates. There are 648 flower seeds. How many flower seeds does each classmate receive?

Section 1.6: Exponential Notation and the Order of Operations Agreement

Objective A: To simplify expressions that contain exponents

Simplify.

81. 3^4

   (A) 34   (B) 81   (C) 27   (D) 12

82. 7^2

   (A) 14   (B) 7   (C) 39   (D) 49

83. $5^2 \cdot 4^2$

   (A) 41   (B) 400   (C) 100   (D) 80

84. $4^7 \cdot 4^5$

   (A) 4^{35} (B) 4^{12} (C) 16^{35} (D) 16^{12}

85. $5^2 \cdot 5^2$

Objective B: To use the Order of Operations Agreement to simplify expressions

Simplify.

86. $3 \cdot (3+9) + 9$

   (A) 45   (B) 27   (C) 63   (D) 324

Simplify.

87. $4 \cdot (20 - 7 + 4)$

    (A) 58   (B) 68   (C) 36   (D) 16

88. $7 \cdot (8 + 3) + 4$

    (A) 81   (B) 105   (C) 308   (D) 63

89. $3 \cdot (2 + 5) - 4$

    (A) 7   (B) 9   (C) 17   (D) 11

90. $8 \cdot (6 + 5) - 2$

Section 1.7 To Factor Numbers

Objective A: To factor numbers

91. Fill in the blank:
_____ is a factor of 20.

    (A) 4   (B) 6   (C) 11   (D) 40

92. Choose the correct statement.

    (A) 3 is a factor of 18.   (B) 10 is a factor of 36.

    (C) 18 is a factor of 3.   (D) 36 is a factor of 10.

93. Which shows all the factors of 30?

    (A) 1, 30   (B) 1, 5, 7, 35   (C) 1, 2, 3, 5, 6, 10, 15, 30   (D) 1, 2, 4, 7, 14, 28, 30

94. Which is *not* a factor of 84?

    (A) 42   (B) 21   (C) 168   (D) 28

95. Write the factors of 20.

Objective B: To find the prime factorization of a number

96. Which shows the prime factorization of 240?

    (A) $2 \cdot 2 \cdot 2 \cdot 2 \cdot 2 \cdot 3 \cdot 5$ (B) $2 \cdot 2 \cdot 2 \cdot 2 \cdot 3 \cdot 7$ (C) $2 \cdot 2 \cdot 2 \cdot 2 \cdot 3 \cdot 5$ (D) none of these

97. Which shows the prime factorization of 990?

    (A) $2 \cdot 2 \cdot 3 \cdot 3 \cdot 5 \cdot 5 \cdot 11$ (B) $2 \cdot 3 \cdot 3 \cdot 5 \cdot 11$ (C) $3 \cdot 3 \cdot 5 \cdot 5 \cdot 10 \cdot 7$ (D) $2 \cdot 3 \cdot 3 \cdot 3 \cdot 5 \cdot 7$

98. Which shows the prime factorization of 44?

    (A) $1 \cdot 2 \cdot 2 \cdot 11$ (B) $2 \cdot 2 \cdot 2 \cdot 11$ (C) $2 \cdot 2 \cdot 11$ (D) $2 \cdot 2 \cdot 11 \cdot 11$

99. Which shows the prime factorization of 225?

    (A) $1 \cdot 3 \cdot 3 \cdot 5 \cdot 5$ (B) $2 \cdot 3 \cdot 3 \cdot 5 \cdot 5$ (C) $3 \cdot 3 \cdot 5 \cdot 5$ (D) $3 \cdot 3 \cdot 5 \cdot 5 \cdot 5$

100. Write the prime factorization of 144.

Chapter 1 Whole Numbers

Section 1.1 Introduction to Whole Numbers

Objective A: To identify the order relation between two numbers

[1] (A) _____

[2] (A) _____

[3] (A) _____

[4] (B) _____

[5] $300,269 < 353,089$ _____

Objective B: To write whole numbers in words and in standard form

[6] (C) _____

[7] (A) _____

[8] (C) _____

[9] (A) _____

[10] five hundred four million, eight hundred fifty-six thousand, nine hundred seven _____

Objective C: To write whole numbers in expanded form

[11] (C) _____

[12] (A) _____

[13] (B) _____

[14] (A) _____

[15] $60,000 + 3000 + 700 + 10 + 3$ _____

Objective D: To round a whole number to a given place value

[16] (D) _____

[17] (D) _____

[18] (A) _____

[19] (A) _____

[20] 40,000 _____

Section 1.2: Addition of Whole Numbers

Objective A: To add whole numbers

[21] (C) _____

[22] (A) _____

[23] (C) _____

[24] (D) _____

[25] 1,225,076 _____

Objective B: To solve application problems

[26] (B) _____

[27] (D) _____

[28] (B) _____

[29] (A)

[30] 6766

Section 1.3: Subtraction of Whole Numbers

Objective A: To subtract whole numbers without borrowing

[31] (A)

[32] (D)

[33] (B)

[34] (C)

[35] 224

Objective B: To subtract whole numbers with borrowing

[36] (C)

[37] (D)

[38] (D)

[39] (D)

[40] 6771

Objective C: To solve application problems

[41] (D)

[42] (C)

[43] (C)

[44] (A)

[45] 17,191,390

Section 1.4: To multiply a number by a single digit

Objective A: To multiply a number by a single digit

[46] (B)

[47] (B)

[48] (C)

[49] (D)

[50] 1300

Objective B: To multiply larger whole numbers

[51] (D)

[52] (B)

[53] (D)

[54] (C)

[55] 3860

Objective C: To solve application problems

[56] (A)

[57] (A) _____

[58] (D) _____

[59] (D) _____

[60] 810 _____

Section 1.5: Division of Whole Numbers

Objective A: To divide by a single digit with no remainders in the quotient

[61] (D) _____

[62] (B) _____

[63] (D) _____

[64] (A) _____

[65] 492 _____

Objective B: To divide by a single digit with a remainder in the quotient

[66] (B) _____

[67] (B) _____

[68] (C) _____

[69] (A) _____

[70] 78 r1 _____

Objective C: To divide by a larger whole number

[71] (B) _____

[72] (B) _____

[73] (B) _____

[74] (C) _____

[75] 67 r34 _____

Objective D: To solve application problems

[76] (D) _____

[77] (B) _____

[78] (A) _____

[79] (A) _____

[80] 24 _____

Section 1.6: Exponential Notation and the Order of Operations Agreement

Objective A: To simplify expressions that contain exponents

[81] (B) _____

[82] (D) _____

[83] (B) _____

[84] (B) _____

[85] 625 _____

Objective B: To use the Order of Operations Agreement to simplify expressions

[86] (A) _____

[87] (C) _____

[88] (A) _____

[89] (C) _____

[90] 86 _____

Section 1.7 To Factor Numbers

Objective A: To factor numbers

[91] (A) _____

[92] (A) _____

[93] (C) _____

[94] (C) _____

[95] 1, 2, 5, 4, 10, 20 _____

Objective B: To find the prime factorization of a number

[96] (C) _____

[97] (B) _____

[98] (C) _____

[99] (C) _____

[100] $2 \cdot 2 \cdot 2 \cdot 2 \cdot 3 \cdot 3$ _____

Chapter 2 Fractions

Section 2.1 The Least Common Multiple and Greatest Common Factor

Objective A: To find the least common multiple (LCM)

Find the least common multiple.

1. 9, 6, and 2
   (A) 108   (B) 17   (C) 1   (D) 18

2. 15, 9, and 16
   (A) 9   (B) 40   (C) 2160   (D) 720

3. 30, 2, and 15
   (A) 47   (B) 2   (C) 900   (D) 30

4. 30 and 18
   (A) 90   (B) 270   (C) 36   (D) 540

5. 6, 4, and 10

Objective B: To find the greatest common factor (GCF)

Find the greatest common factor.

6. 60 and 40
   (A) 30   (B) 20   (C) 120   (D) none of these

7. 12 and 8
   (A) 4   (B) 8   (C) 6   (D) 2

8. 54, 36, and 90
   (A) 36   (B) 6   (C) 18   (D) 12

9. 63, 126, and 84
   (A) 21   (B) 3   (C) 36   (D) 12

10. 140, 520, and 460

Section 2.2: Introduction to Fractions

Objective A: To write a fraction that represents part of a whole

11. Which fraction of the rectangle is shaded?

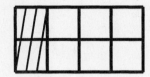

(A) $\dfrac{8}{2}$ (B) $\dfrac{2}{16}$ (C) $\dfrac{6}{8}$ (D) $\dfrac{2}{8}$

12. Which fraction of the circle is shaded?

(A) $\dfrac{8}{4}$ (B) $\dfrac{4}{8}$ (C) $\dfrac{7}{8}$ (D) $\dfrac{8}{7}$

13. Which fraction of the bar is shaded?

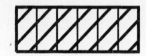

(A) $\dfrac{0}{6}$ (B) $\dfrac{6}{6}$ (C) $\dfrac{1}{6}$ (D) $\dfrac{6}{0}$

14. Which model below shows $\dfrac{5}{6}$ shaded?

(A)    (B)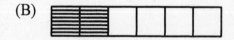

(C) 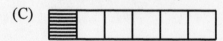   (D)

15. What fraction of the circle is shaded?

Objective B: To write an improper fraction as a mixed number or a whole number, and a mixed number as an improper fraction

16. Which shows $8\frac{1}{2}$ as an improper fraction?

   (A) $\frac{16}{2}$ (B) $\frac{17}{2}$ (C) $\frac{15}{2}$ (D) $\frac{81}{2}$

17. Which shows $2\frac{3}{7}$ as in improper fraction?

   (A) $\frac{17}{7}$ (B) $\frac{7}{42}$ (C) $\frac{42}{7}$ (D) $\frac{7}{17}$

18. Which shows $\frac{25}{6}$ as a mixed number?

   (A) $25\frac{1}{6}$ (B) $1\frac{6}{19}$ (C) $4\frac{1}{6}$ (D) $\frac{1}{6}$

19. Which shows $\frac{34}{5}$ as a mixed number?

   (A) $1\frac{6}{5}$ (B) $6\frac{4}{5}$ (C) $1\frac{7}{5}$ (D) $6\frac{5}{4}$

20. Write $8\frac{1}{2}$ as an improper fraction.

Section 2.3: Writing Equivalent Fractions

Objective A: To find equivalent fractions by raising to higher terms

21. Which is a fraction equivalent to $\frac{1}{3}$ with a denominator of 30?

    (A) $\frac{10}{30}$ (B) $\frac{11}{30}$ (C) $\frac{8}{30}$ (D) $\frac{12}{30}$

22. Which of the following fractions is equivalent to $\frac{6}{7}$?

    (A) $\frac{54}{63}$ (B) $\frac{54}{84}$ (C) $\frac{7}{6}$ (D) $\frac{72}{63}$

23. Which of the following fractions is equivalent to $\frac{1}{5}$?

    (A) $\frac{5}{1}$ (B) $\frac{3}{25}$ (C) $\frac{5}{15}$ (D) $\frac{5}{25}$

24. Which of the following fractions is equivalent to $\frac{15}{13}$?

    (A) $\frac{120}{91}$ (B) $\frac{26}{75}$ (C) $\frac{45}{39}$ (D) $\frac{90}{65}$

25. Find a fraction equivalent to $\frac{2}{5}$ with a denominator of 20.

Objective B: To write a fraction in simplest form

26. Which shows $\frac{30}{40}$ in simplest form?

    (A) $\frac{3}{4}$ (B) 10   (C) $\frac{4}{3}$ (D) 30

27. Which shows $\dfrac{8}{12}$ in simplest form?

    (A) $\dfrac{9}{11}$ (B) $\dfrac{80}{120}$ (C) $\dfrac{6}{5}$ (D) $\dfrac{2}{3}$

28. Which shows $\dfrac{48}{60}$ in simplest form?

    (A) $\dfrac{4}{15}$ (B) $\dfrac{16}{20}$ (C) $\dfrac{4}{5}$ (D) $\dfrac{12}{15}$

29. Which shows $\dfrac{6}{12}$ in simplest form?

    (A) $\dfrac{1}{6}$ (B) $\dfrac{2}{4}$ (C) 6   (D) $\dfrac{1}{2}$

30. Write $\dfrac{10}{20}$ in simplest form.

Section 2.4: Addition of Fractions and Mixed Numbers

Objective A: To add fractions with the same denominator

Add.

31. $\dfrac{2}{14} + \dfrac{9}{14}$

    (A) $\dfrac{11}{14}$ (B) $1\dfrac{3}{7}$ (C) $\dfrac{5}{7}$ (D) $1\dfrac{3}{11}$

32. $\dfrac{11}{12} + \dfrac{5}{12}$

    (A) $1\dfrac{1}{3}$ (B) $\dfrac{2}{3}$ (C) $1\dfrac{5}{12}$ (D) $1\dfrac{1}{2}$

Add.

33. $\dfrac{5}{19} + \dfrac{2}{19} + \dfrac{1}{19} + \dfrac{3}{19}$

    (A) $\dfrac{11}{76}$ (B) $\dfrac{10}{19}$ (C) $\dfrac{11}{19}$ (D) $\dfrac{13}{76}$

34. $\dfrac{1}{6} + \dfrac{2}{6} + \dfrac{4}{6}$

    (A) $\dfrac{7}{12}$ (B) $\dfrac{1}{2}$ (C) $1\dfrac{1}{6}$ (D) none of these

35. $\dfrac{9}{11} + \dfrac{6}{11} + \dfrac{4}{11} + \dfrac{8}{11}$

Objective B: To add fractions with unlike denominators

Add.

36. $\dfrac{2}{5} + \dfrac{1}{15}$

    (A) $\dfrac{7}{15}$ (B) $2\dfrac{1}{7}$ (C) $\dfrac{1}{25}$ (D) $\dfrac{3}{20}$

37. $\dfrac{1}{2} + \dfrac{9}{10}$

    (A) $\dfrac{5}{6}$ (B) $\dfrac{1}{2}$ (C) $\dfrac{5}{7}$ (D) $1\dfrac{2}{5}$

38. $\dfrac{5}{6} + \dfrac{1}{10}$

    (A) $\dfrac{3}{8}$ (B) $\dfrac{14}{15}$ (C) $\dfrac{1}{10}$ (D) $\dfrac{1}{5}$

Add.

39. $\dfrac{1}{15} + \dfrac{1}{20}$

    (A) $\dfrac{2}{15}$ (B) $\dfrac{1}{300}$ (C) $\dfrac{7}{60}$ (D) $\dfrac{2}{35}$

40. $\dfrac{1}{8} + \dfrac{7}{16}$

Objective C: To add whole numbers, mixed numbers, and fractions

Add.

41. $3\dfrac{1}{2} + 2\dfrac{1}{2}$

    (A) 5 (B) 6 (C) $5\dfrac{1}{2}$ (D) $6\dfrac{1}{2}$

42. $5\dfrac{10}{19} + 3\dfrac{4}{19}$

    (A) $2\dfrac{3}{19}$ (B) $\dfrac{6}{19}$ (C) $3\dfrac{6}{19}$ (D) $8\dfrac{14}{19}$

43. $2\dfrac{3}{7} + 6\dfrac{6}{7}$

    (A) $10\dfrac{2}{7}$ (B) $9\dfrac{3}{7}$ (C) $10\dfrac{3}{7}$ (D) $9\dfrac{2}{7}$

44. $6\dfrac{1}{4} + 2$

    (A) $8\dfrac{1}{4}$ (B) $6\dfrac{3}{4}$ (C) $6\dfrac{1}{6}$ (D) $4\dfrac{1}{4}$

45. $3\dfrac{1}{3} + 3$

Objective D: To solve application problems

46. A pattern for a wedding outfit calls for $14\frac{2}{3}$ yards of lace trim for the dress and $9\frac{3}{5}$ yards of lace trim for the veil. How many yards of lace trim does the pattern call for?

(A) $15\frac{4}{15}$ (B) $24\frac{4}{5}$ (C) $27\frac{7}{15}$ (D) none of these

47. Tina has $\frac{2}{3}$ of a bottle of juice, Peggy has $\frac{5}{6}$ of a bottle of juice, and Mary has $\frac{1}{2}$ of a bottle of juice. How many bottles of juice do they have all together?

(A) 2   (B) $1\frac{5}{6}$ (C) $\frac{7}{11}$ (D) $\frac{8}{11}$

48. Patricia, Clark, and Pandora were assigned a group project. Working independently, Patricia spent $4\frac{1}{2}$ hours, Clark spent $7\frac{1}{2}$ hours, and Pandora spent $2\frac{5}{8}$ hours. They also spent $5\frac{3}{8}$ hours working together. How much time was put towards the project?

(A) 40 hr   (B) $16\frac{1}{4}$ hr   (C) $19\frac{5}{8}$ hr   (D) 20 hr

49. Gadget Manufacturing had stock that sold at a price of $32\frac{1}{8}$ points. The stock rose $5\frac{1}{4}$ points. Which is the new price?

(A) 37 points   (B) $37\frac{5}{16}$ points   (C) $37\frac{7}{16}$ points   (D) $37\frac{3}{8}$ points

50. Frank has three sacks of peanuts. One of the sacks contains 3 pounds, one contains $\frac{1}{14}$ pounds, and one contains $4\frac{2}{7}$ pounds. How many pounds of peanuts does Frank have in all?

Section 2.5: Subtraction of Fractions and Mixed Numbers

Objective A: To subtract fractions with the same denominator

Subtract.

51. $\dfrac{11}{13} - \dfrac{8}{13}$

    (A) 3   (B) $\dfrac{3}{13}$ (C) $\dfrac{4}{13}$ (D) $1\dfrac{6}{13}$

52. $\dfrac{19}{30} - \dfrac{13}{30}$

    (A) $\dfrac{1}{10}$ (B) $\dfrac{1}{12}$ (C) $\dfrac{1}{5}$ (D) $\dfrac{4}{15}$

53. $\dfrac{13}{17} - \dfrac{12}{17}$

    (A) $1\dfrac{8}{17}$ (B) 1   (C) $\dfrac{1}{17}$ (D) $\dfrac{2}{17}$

54. $\dfrac{7}{5} - \dfrac{4}{5}$

    (A) 3   (B) $\dfrac{3}{5}$ (C) $\dfrac{11}{5}$ (D) none of these

55. $\dfrac{20}{7} - \dfrac{17}{7}$

Objective B: To subtract fractions with unlike denominators

Subtract.

56. $\dfrac{11}{12} - \dfrac{1}{7}$

    (A) $\dfrac{89}{84}$ (B) $\dfrac{11}{84}$ (C) $\dfrac{65}{84}$ (D) none of these

Subtract.

57. $\dfrac{7}{8} - \dfrac{13}{16}$

(A) $\dfrac{5}{64}$ (B) $\dfrac{9}{128}$ (C) 1 (D) $\dfrac{1}{16}$

58. $\dfrac{6}{7} - \dfrac{1}{4}$

(A) $\dfrac{31}{28}$ (B) $\dfrac{17}{28}$ (C) $\dfrac{5}{28}$ (D) none of these

59. $\dfrac{2}{3} - \dfrac{3}{9}$

(A) $\dfrac{1}{6}$ (B) $\dfrac{1}{12}$ (C) $\dfrac{1}{3}$ (D) $\dfrac{5}{12}$

60. $\dfrac{24}{25} - \dfrac{11}{30}$

Objective C: To subtract whole numbers, mixed numbers, and fractions

Subtract.

61. $\dfrac{2}{3} - \dfrac{1}{9}$

(A) $\dfrac{2}{27}$ (B) $\dfrac{7}{9}$ (C) $\dfrac{1}{27}$ (D) $\dfrac{5}{9}$

62. $6 - 1\dfrac{3}{5}$

(A) $5\dfrac{2}{5}$ (B) $4\dfrac{2}{5}$ (C) $7\dfrac{3}{5}$ (D) none of these

Subtract.

63. $5 - 4\dfrac{5}{6}$

    (A) $9\dfrac{5}{6}$ (B) $\dfrac{1}{6}$ (C) $1\dfrac{5}{6}$ (D) $4\dfrac{1}{6}$

64. $6\dfrac{3}{8} - 1\dfrac{1}{5}$

    (A) $5\dfrac{7}{40}$ (B) $5\dfrac{2}{3}$ (C) $\dfrac{3}{40}$ (D) none of these

65. $3 - 2\dfrac{1}{2}$

Objective D: To solve application problems

66. Aaron had $4\dfrac{5}{8}$ pounds of potting soil and used $1\dfrac{3}{4}$ pounds of it. How much potting soil did Aaron have left?

    (A) $2\dfrac{7}{8}$ lb   (B) $2\dfrac{27}{32}$ lb   (C) $3\dfrac{1}{2}$ lb   (D) none of these

67. The width of a dining room window is $\dfrac{7}{8}$ yard. Romeo bought a wood frame that is $\dfrac{3}{4}$ yard wide. Find the difference in widths. If the frame should be wider than the window, does the frame fit?

    (A) $\dfrac{7}{32}$ yd; Yes   (B) $1\dfrac{13}{32}$ yd; Yes   (C) $1\dfrac{5}{8}$ yd; No   (D) $\dfrac{1}{8}$ yd; No

68. Sam and Martha decided to have a contest to find who could read more per week. Sam read for $14\dfrac{1}{2}$ hours, and Martha read for $11\dfrac{3}{4}$ hours. How much more did Sam read?

    (A) $2\dfrac{1}{2}$ hr   (B) $2\dfrac{3}{4}$ hr   (C) $3\dfrac{3}{4}$ hr   (D) $2\dfrac{1}{4}$ hr

69. Gi-Young made a triple batch of molasses cookies. She used $7\frac{3}{4}$ cups of flour. Before she made her cookies she had $8\frac{1}{8}$ cups of flour. How much flour does Gi-Young have left?

(A) $\frac{3}{8}$ cups

(B) $15\frac{7}{8}$ cups

(C) $15\frac{15}{16}$ cups

(D) $\frac{7}{16}$ cups

70. Three holes are drilled into a metal sash. What is the distance from the center of hole Y to the center of hole Z?

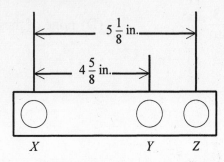

Section 2.6: Multiplication of Fractions and Mixed Numbers

Objective A: To multiply fractions

Multiply.

71. $\frac{15}{13} \times \frac{11}{3}$

(A) $2\frac{7}{13}$

(B) $\frac{2}{3}$

(C) $4\frac{3}{13}$

(D) $9\frac{8}{15}$

72. $\frac{1}{3} \times \frac{4}{5}$

(A) $\frac{8}{13}$

(B) $\frac{5}{12}$

(C) $\frac{80}{3}$

(D) $\frac{4}{15}$

73. $\frac{3}{7} \times \frac{6}{7}$

(A) $\frac{18}{7}$

(B) $\frac{18}{49}$

(C) $\frac{9}{49}$

(D) none of these

Multiply.

74. $\dfrac{1}{3} \times \dfrac{6}{7}$

(A) $\dfrac{7}{10}$ (B) $\dfrac{7}{18}$ (C) $\dfrac{9}{8}$ (D) none of these

75. $\dfrac{8}{5} \times \dfrac{3}{4}$

Objective B: To multiply whole numbers, mixed numbers, and fractions

Multiply.

76. $5\dfrac{1}{2} \times \dfrac{1}{4}$

(A) $1\dfrac{3}{8}$ (B) $\dfrac{1}{8}$ (C) $\dfrac{3}{4}$ (D) none of these

77. $\dfrac{1}{4} \times 3\dfrac{1}{4}$

(A) $3\dfrac{1}{2}$ (B) $\dfrac{13}{16}$ (C) $\dfrac{7}{8}$ (D) $\dfrac{13}{17}$

78. $6\dfrac{1}{4} \times \dfrac{1}{2}$

(A) $\dfrac{7}{8}$ (B) $3\dfrac{5}{8}$ (C) $3\dfrac{1}{8}$ (D) $2\dfrac{7}{8}$

79. $\dfrac{5}{7} \times 9\dfrac{1}{7}$

(A) $6\dfrac{26}{49}$ (B) $3\dfrac{8}{9}$ (C) $\dfrac{5}{49}$ (D) $\dfrac{1}{7}$

80. $\dfrac{5}{6} \times 8\dfrac{1}{3}$

Objective C: To solve application problems

81. In the same length of time, Barbara can complete $\frac{5}{8}$ of the work that Eric and Barry can complete working together. If Eric can do $\frac{1}{3}$ of a job in three hours and Barry can do $\frac{1}{4}$ of the same job in three hours, how much of the job can Barbara do in three hours?

(A) $\frac{14}{15}$ (B) $\frac{5}{44}$ (C) $\frac{5}{96}$ (D) $\frac{35}{96}$

82. At a warehouse, boxes of merchandise are placed on shelves in stacks that are 14 boxes high. If each box is $19\frac{3}{4}$ inches in height, how tall is the stack of boxes?

(A) $276\frac{1}{2}$ in.   (B) $266\frac{3}{4}$ in.   (C) 280 in.   (D) $274\frac{1}{8}$ in.

83. Harriet had $5\frac{3}{5}$ sacks of cement and used $\frac{3}{7}$ of it. How much cement did Harriet use?

(A) $2\frac{2}{5}$ sacks   (B) $\frac{3}{7}$ sack   (C) $11\frac{2}{3}$ sacks   (D) $2\frac{8}{15}$ sacks

84. Enrique found a board to make a shelf. It was $6\frac{2}{3}$ feet long. He needed $\frac{1}{2}$ of it for the shelf. How long was the shelf?

(A) $3\frac{1}{3}$ ft   (B) 3 ft   (C) $3\frac{1}{2}$ ft   (D) $6\frac{1}{6}$ ft

85. Jimmy made a patio using $4\frac{5}{6}$ bags of cement. He wants to make another patio that will be $3\frac{1}{8}$ times as large as the first. How many bags of cement will Jimmy need?

Section 1.7 Division of Fractions and Mixed Numbers

Objective A: To divide fractions

Divide.

86. $\dfrac{10}{3} \div \dfrac{4}{5}$

(A) $1\dfrac{3}{4}$ (B) $4\dfrac{1}{6}$ (C) $1\dfrac{1}{2}$ (D) $1\dfrac{2}{3}$

87. $\dfrac{2}{7} \div \dfrac{14}{7}$

(A) $\dfrac{4}{7}$ (B) $\dfrac{1}{7}$ (C) $\dfrac{1}{2}$ (D) 2

88. $\dfrac{4}{15} \div \dfrac{1}{3}$

(A) $1\dfrac{1}{4}$ (B) $\dfrac{1}{4}$ (C) $\dfrac{4}{45}$ (D) $\dfrac{4}{5}$

89. $\dfrac{2}{3} \div \dfrac{18}{7}$

(A) $\dfrac{7}{54}$ (B) $3\dfrac{5}{21}$ (C) $1\dfrac{5}{7}$ (D) $\dfrac{7}{27}$

90. $\dfrac{2}{9} \div \dfrac{18}{3}$

Objective B: To divide whole numbers, mixed numbers, and fractions

Divide.

91. $2\dfrac{3}{8} \div 1\dfrac{3}{4}$

(A) $5\dfrac{13}{24}$ (B) $1\dfrac{5}{14}$ (C) $\dfrac{14}{19}$ (D) 1

Divide.

92. $3\dfrac{4}{9} \div \dfrac{9}{4}$

    (A) $1\dfrac{43}{81}$ (B) $7\dfrac{3}{4}$ (C) $1\dfrac{7}{9}$ (D) none of these

93. $28 \div \dfrac{2}{7}$

    (A) $\dfrac{1}{98}$ (B) 98   (C) 28   (D) none of these

94. $\dfrac{5}{3} \div 15$

    (A) $\dfrac{1}{25}$ (B) $\dfrac{1}{9}$ (C) $\dfrac{1}{5}$ (D) none of these

95. $7 \div 1\dfrac{1}{4}$

Objective C: To solve application problems

96. A new custodian cleaned $\dfrac{1}{8}$ of a classroom in ten minutes, which was only $\dfrac{6}{7}$ of what an experienced custodian could do. What part of a room could an experienced custodian clean in ten minutes?

    (A) $1\dfrac{1}{4}$ (B) $\dfrac{7}{48}$ (C) $\dfrac{3}{28}$ (D) $8\dfrac{4}{7}$

97. Bane spent 1 hour on his homework. He spent an equal amount of time on each subject. If Bane spent $\dfrac{1}{3}$ hour on reading, how many subjects did he study?

    (A) 4   (B) 3   (C) 5   (D) 2

98. Kevin was wallpapering the bedroom. The pattern of the wallpaper was repeated vertically every $\frac{1}{2}$ foot. If the portion being wallpapered was 10 feet tall, how many times was the pattern repeated?

(A) 22   (B) 20   (C) 14   (D) 12

99. The top walking deck of a sail boat is $13\frac{1}{7}$ feet long. If this is only $\frac{19}{21}$ of the length of the boat, how long is the boat?

(A) $13\frac{10}{19}$ ft   (B) $14\frac{10}{19}$ ft   (C) $14\frac{9}{19}$ ft   (D) $14\frac{14}{19}$ ft

100. It took $6\frac{1}{2}$ gallons of gas to fill the tank of the family car. If the tank was $\frac{1}{4}$ full when they arrived at the gas station, how much gas does the tank hold?

Section 2.8 Order, Exponents, and the Order of Operations Agreement

Objective A: To identify the order of relation between two fractions

Choose the correct symbol, >,<, or =.

101. $\frac{6}{7}$ —— $\frac{1}{2}$

(A) >   (B) <   (C) =

102. $\frac{2}{9}$ —— $\frac{1}{2}$

(A) >   (B) <   (C) =

103. $\frac{5}{14}$ —— $\frac{5}{4}$

(A) >   (B) <   (C) =

104. $\frac{3}{4}$ —— $\frac{3}{4}$

(A) >   (B) <   (C) =

105. Insert the correct symbol, >,<, or =, between the two fractions. $\dfrac{7}{8}$ ____ $\dfrac{1}{4}$

Objective B: To simplify expressions containing exponents

Simplify.

106. $\left(\dfrac{2}{3}\right)^2$

    (A) $\dfrac{4}{9}$ (B) $\dfrac{2}{3}$ (C) $\dfrac{2}{5}$ (D) $\dfrac{4}{3}$

107. $\left(\dfrac{4}{5}\right)^2$

    (A) $\dfrac{8}{25}$ (B) $\dfrac{2}{9}$ (C) $\dfrac{16}{25}$ (D) $\dfrac{16}{5}$

108. $\left(\dfrac{4}{3}\right)^2 \cdot \left(\dfrac{1}{16}\right)$

    (A) $\dfrac{4}{48}$ (B) $\dfrac{1}{6}$ (C) $\dfrac{16}{9}$ (D) $\dfrac{1}{9}$

109. $\left(\dfrac{3}{5}\right)^2 \cdot \left(\dfrac{1}{9}\right)$

    (A) $\dfrac{1}{10}$ (B) $\dfrac{9}{25}$ (C) $\dfrac{1}{25}$ (D) $\dfrac{3}{45}$

110. $\left(\dfrac{1}{2}\right)^2 \cdot \left(\dfrac{3}{5}\right)^3$

Objective C: To use the Order of Operations Agreement to simplify expressions

Simplify.

111. $\dfrac{1}{3} \cdot \left(\dfrac{1}{4} + \dfrac{1}{3} \right)$

    (A) $\dfrac{7}{36}$ (B) $\dfrac{1}{3}$ (C) $\dfrac{1}{6}$ (D) $1\dfrac{1}{3}$

112. $\left(\dfrac{1}{5} + \dfrac{5}{6} \right)\left(\dfrac{7}{30} - \dfrac{1}{5} \right)$

    (A) $1\dfrac{1}{15}$ (B) $\dfrac{31}{900}$ (C) $\dfrac{403}{900}$ (D) $\dfrac{7}{36}$

113. $\dfrac{4}{7} + 5\left(\dfrac{4}{6} + 4 \right)$

    (A) $23\dfrac{19}{21}$ (B) $23\dfrac{5}{6}$ (C) $7\dfrac{19}{21}$ (D) $7\dfrac{41}{42}$

114. $\left(\dfrac{1}{5} + \dfrac{3}{4} \right)\left(\dfrac{13}{20} - \dfrac{1}{5} \right)$

    (A) $\dfrac{39}{80}$ (B) $\dfrac{323}{400}$ (C) $1\dfrac{2}{5}$ (D) $\dfrac{171}{400}$

115. $\left(\dfrac{9}{4} \right)^2 - 2\dfrac{3}{4} \cdot 1\dfrac{3}{4}$

Chapter 2 Fractions

Section 2.1 The Least Common Multiple and Greatest Common Factor

Objective A: To find the least common multiple (LCM)

[1] (D)

[2] (D)

[3] (D)

[4] (A)

[5] 60

Objective B: To find the greatest common factor (GCF)

[6] (B)

[7] (A)

[8] (C)

[9] (A)

[10] 20

Section 2.2: Introduction to Fractions

Objective A: To write a fraction that represents part of a whole

[11] (D)

[12] (C)

[13] (B)

[14] (A) _____

[15] $\dfrac{5}{8}$ _____

Objective B: To write an improper fraction as a mixed number or a whole number, and a mixed number as an improper fraction

[16] (B) _____

[17] (A) _____

[18] (C) _____

[19] (B) _____

[20] $\dfrac{17}{2}$ _____

Section 2.3: Writing Equivalent Fractions

Objective A: To find equivalent fractions by raising to higher terms

[21] (A) _____

[22] (A) _____

[23] (D) _____

[24] (C) _____

[25] $\dfrac{8}{20}$ _____

Objective B: To write a fraction in simplest form

[26] (A) _____

[27] (D) _____

[28] (C) _____

[29] (D) _____

[30] $\dfrac{1}{2}$ _____

Section 2.4: Addition of Fractions and Mixed Numbers

Objective A: To add fractions with the same denominator

[31] (A) _____

[32] (A) _____

[33] (C) _____

[34] (C) _____

[35] $2\dfrac{5}{11}$ _____

Objective B: To add fractions with unlike denominators

[36] (A) _____

[37] (D) _____

[38] (B) _____

[39] (C)

[40] $\dfrac{9}{16}$

Objective C: To add whole numbers, mixed numbers, and fractions

[41] (B)

[42] (D)

[43] (D)

[44] (A)

[45] $6\dfrac{1}{3}$

Objective D: To solve application problems

[46] (D)

[47] (A)

[48] (D)

[49] (D)

[50] $7\dfrac{5}{14}$ lb

Section 2.5: Subtraction of Fractions and Mixed Numbers

Objective A: To subtract fractions with the same denominator

[51] (B)

[52] (C) _____

[53] (C) _____

[54] (B) _____

[55] $\dfrac{3}{7}$ _____

Objective B: To subtract fractions with unlike denominators

[56] (C) _____

[57] (D) _____

[58] (B) _____

[59] (C) _____

[60] $\dfrac{89}{150}$ _____

Objective C: To subtract whole numbers, mixed numbers, and fractions

[61] (D) _____

[62] (B) _____

[63] (B) _____

[64] (A) _____

[65] $\dfrac{1}{2}$ _____

Objective D: To solve application problems

[66] (A) _____

[67] (D) _____

[68] (B) _____

[69] (A) _____

[70] $\dfrac{1}{2}$ in. _____

Section 2.6: Multiplication of Fractions and Mixed Numbers

Objective A: To multiply fractions

[71] (C) _____

[72] (D) _____

[73] (B) _____

[74] (D) _____

[75] $1\dfrac{1}{5}$ _____

Objective B: To multiply whole numbers, mixed numbers, and fractions

[76] (A) _____

[77] (B) _____

[78] (C) _____

[79] (A) _____

[80] $6\dfrac{17}{18}$ _____

Objective C: To solve application problems

[81] (D) _____

[82] (A) _____

[83] (A) _____

[84] (A) _____

[85] $15\dfrac{5}{48}$ _____

Section 1.7 Division of Fractions and Mixed Numbers

Objective A: To divide fractions

[86] (B) _____

[87] (B) _____

[88] (D) _____

[89] (D) _____

[90] $\dfrac{1}{27}$ _____

Objective B: To divide whole numbers, mixed numbers, and fractions

[91] (B) _____

[92] (A) _____

[93] (B) _____

[94] (B) _____

[95] $5\dfrac{3}{5}$ _____

Objective C: To solve application problems

[96] (B) _____

[97] (B) _____

[98] (B) _____

[99] (B) _____

[100] $8\dfrac{2}{3}$ gal _____

Section 2.8 Order, Exponents, and the Order of Operations Agreement

Objective A: To identify the order of relation between two fractions

[101] (A) _____

[102] (B) _____

[103] (A) _____

[104] (C) _____

[105] $\dfrac{7}{8} > \dfrac{1}{4}$ _____

Objective B: To simplify expressions containing exponents

[106] (A) _____

[107] (C) _____

[108] (D) _____

[109] (C) _____

[110] $\dfrac{27}{500}$ _____

Objective C: To use the Order of Operations Agreement to simplify expressions

[111] (A) _____

[112] (B) _____

[113] (A) _____

[114] (D) _____

[115] $\dfrac{1}{4}$ _____

Chapter 3 Decimals

Section 3.1 Introduction to Decimals

Objective A: To write decimals in standard form and in words

1. Which is the word name for 4.3?

   (A) forty-three

   (B) four and three tenths

   (C) three and four tenths

   (D) forty-three hundredths

2. Which is the word name for 0.43?

   (A) forty-three hundredths

   (B) forty and three thousandths

   (C) forty and three hundredths

   (D) forty-three thousandths

3. Which is the decimal in standard form?
   one hundred five and nine tenths

   (A) 105.9   (B) 1050.9   (C) 105.910   (D) 105.09

4. Which is the decimal in standard form?
   three thousand five hundred one and eighty-four hundredths

   (A) 30,501.84   (B) 3051.84   (C) 3501.84   (D) 3501.084

5. Write the word name for 433.61.

Objective B: To round a decimal to a given place value

6. Round 5.338 to the nearest tenth.

   (A) 5.3   (B) 5.4   (C) 5.34   (D) 5.35

7. Round 85.267 to the nearest tenth.

   (A) 85.4   (B) 85.3   (C) 85.1   (D) 85.5

8. Round 0.891367 to the nearest hundredth.

   (A) 0.892   (B) 0.89   (C) 0.891   (D) 0.90

9. Round 22.313 to the nearest hundredth.

   (A) 22.31   (B) 0.31   (C) 22.32   (D) 22.30

10. Round 37.784 to the nearest hundredth.

Section 3.2: Addition of Decimals

Objective A: To add decimals

Add.

11.   20.69
    8.22
+ 1.3

   (A) 28.91   (B) 30.21   (C) 21.99   (D) 9.52

12.   12.93
    4.41
+ 10.3

   (A) 27.64   (B) 37.94   (C) 14.71   (D) 23.23

13. $761.903 + 754.830$

   (A) 1524.860   (B) 1517.733   (C) 1524.203   (D) 1516.733

14. $56.454 + 3.69$

   (A) 568.23   (B) 60.144   (C) 63.654   (D) 56.823

15. $15.32 + 479.741 + 3.4167$

Objective B: To solve application problems

16. Lee added 1.123 grams of one chemical to 2.226 grams of water. How many total grams did Lee have?

   (A) 2.349   (B) 3.339   (C) 33.49   (D) 3.349

17. Veronica has 3 packages to mail. The packages weigh 2.06 pounds, 2.00 pounds and 2.81 pounds. What is the total weight of Veronica's packages?

   (A) 6.87 lb   (B) 4.06 lb   (C) 4.87 lb   (D) 4.81 lb

18. In a three-person medley relay race, the 100 meter was run in 10.34 seconds, the 200 meter in 20.53 seconds, and the 400 meter in 45.48 seconds. Which was the total time for the race?

    (A) 76.45 s   (B) 76.35 s   (C) 77.35 s   (D) 25.45 s

19. Ruth has four strings. One is 16.88 centimeters long, one is 34.74 centimeters long, one is 63.66 centimeters long and one is 18.4 centimeters long. How many centimeters of string does she have in all?

    (A) 133.68   (B) 114.28   (C) 115.28   (D) 135.09

20. Neil ordered a wallet for $13.77, a sweater for $22.87, and a watch for $82.14 from a mail-order catalog. He added $15.32 for tax, shipping, and handling. What was the total cost of Neil's order?

Section 3.3: Subtraction of Decimals

Objective A: To subtract decimals

Subtract.

21.   27.26
     − 9.13

    (A) 17.53   (B) 18.13   (C) 36.39   (D) 35.99

22.   6.5
     − 2.82

    (A) 9.22   (B) 3.69   (C) 3.68   (D) 9.32

23. 348.64 − 19.4

    (A) 154.64   (B) 368.04   (C) 346.7   (D) 329.24

24. 13.84 − 1.597

    (A) 11.243   (B) 11.487   (C) 13.243   (D) 12.243

25. 547.31 − 18.9

Objective B: To solve application problems

26. Manny had $76.55 in his checking account. He wrote a check for $23.69. How much money did he have left in the account?

(A) $52.86   (B) $51.86   (C) $100.24   (D) $101.24

27. In the 1988 Olympics, the winning time for the women's 100-meter race was 11.06 seconds. The winning time of the men's race was 10.25 seconds. How much faster was the men's time?

(A) 20.31 s   (B) 0.19 s   (C) 21.31 s   (D) 0.81 s

28. Meg has 2 milligrams of iron and 0.17 milligrams of silicon. How much more iron does she have than silicon?

(A) 2.17 mg   (B) 1.73 mg   (C) 1.83 mg   (D) 18.3 mg

29. Patrick and his sister went fishing. Patrick caught a 10.5-inch fish and his sister caught an 11.7-inch fish. How much longer was his sister's fish?

(A) 1.2 in.   (B) 22.1 in.   (C) 1.1 in.   (D) 22.2 in.

30. Nan has saved $270.51 toward the purchase of a recorder that costs $1696.80. How much more must Nan save in order to buy the recorder?

Section 4.4: Multiplication of Decimals

Objective A: To multiply decimals

Multiply.

31.   173
       × 0.017

(A) 294.1   (B) 29.41   (C) 2.941   (D) 0.2941

32.   8.005
       × 0.016

(A) 0.12808   (B) 1.288   (C) 1.2808   (D) 8.4853

33. 0.06×5.5

(A) 0.33   (B) 0.033   (C) 3.3   (D) 0.0033

Multiply.

34. 58.7×0.013

(A) 7.631   (B) 0.07631   (C) 763.1   (D) 0.7631

35. 3.007
$\times$ 0.078

Objective B: To solve application problems

36. Listed below are the prices of the Sudsy Wudsy Laundromat.

Wash per load	$0.60
Dry per load	$1.35
Soap	$0.90
Bleach	$0.85

George washes and dries 5 loads and buys 4 boxes of soap and a box of bleach. How much does George spend?

(A) $7.45   (B) $11.20   (C) $14.20   (D) $13.35

37. Renee reports that on her last trip abroad, the Japanese Yen (¥) was worth $0.0106. She bought souvenirs which cost ¥3250. How much did they cost in US dollars?

(A) $34.45   (B) $3.45   (C) $344.50   (D) $0.34

38. A car rental costs $11.95 a day plus $0.30 a mile. If Chloe rents the car for 2 days and drives 460 miles, what is her cost?

(A) $79.67   (B) $138.00   (C) $23.90   (D) $161.90

39. On Tara's first trip as a commercial truck driver, fuel cost $1.36 a gallon. Tara averaged 7 miles to a gallon of fuel. How much did the gasoline cost for her trip of 385 miles?

(A) $74.80   (B) $55.00   (C) $9.52   (D) $523.60

40. Mrs. Berry drove a tractor-trailer throughout the state of Texas. If fuel cost $1.37 a gallon and Mrs. Berry averaged 5 miles to a gallon of fuel, how much did the gasoline cost for her trip of 200 miles?

Section 3.5: Division of Decimals

Objective A: To divide decimals

Divide.

41. $1.44 \div 0.04$

    (A) 3.6   (B) 360   (C) 36   (D) 0.036

42. $5.85 \div 1.3$

    (A) 4.5   (B) 3.5   (C) 4.6   (D) 3.4

43. $297.6 \div 24$

    (A) 11.4   (B) 12.4   (C) 1.24   (D) 114

44. $0.4 \overline{)3.04}$

    (A) 7.6   (B) 0.76   (C) 0.706   (D) 12.6

45. $0.19 \overline{)6.65}$

Objective B: To solve application problems

46. Audrey bought 16.1 quarts of liquid soap for a total of $19.00. Which was the price per quart of liquid soap?

    (A) $0.12   (B) $1.18   (C) $1.09   (D) none of these

47. Brendan sells roses for $11.99 a bunch. At the end of the day he had collected $167.86. How many bunches of roses did he sell?

    (A) 14   (B) 10   (C) 15   (D) 11

48. Each story of a building is 17.4 meters tall. If the height of the building is 295.8 meters, how many floors does the building have?

    (A) 17   (B) 13   (C) 18   (D) 16

49. A clothing manufacturer had 676 meters of fabric to make identical dresses, all of the same size. If each dress used 2.6 meters of fabric, how many dresses could be made?

    (A) 1758   (B) 681   (C) 26   (D) 260

50. A charter bus holding 85 passengers costs $59.50 an hour. If a round trip took 5 hours, what did it cost each passenger?

Objective A: To convert fractions to decimals

51. Which shows $2\frac{3}{8}$ as a decimal?

   (A) 0.203   (B) 2.03   (C) 2.375   (D) 2.67

52. Which shows $\frac{17}{20}$ as a decimal?

   (A) 0.85   (B) 1.17647   (C) 17.00   (D) 0.22

53. Which shows $\frac{2}{11}$ as a decimal?

   (A) 0.18   (B) $0.\overline{181}$ (C) $0.1\overline{8}$ (D) $0.\overline{18}$

54. Which shows $5\frac{5}{8}$ as a decimal?

   (A) 5.625   (B) 4.375   (C) 0.625   (D) 1.25

55. Write $\frac{1}{25}$ as a decimal.

Objective B: To convert decimals to fractions

56. Which shows 0.6875 as a reduced fraction?

   (A) $\frac{11}{160}$ (B) $6\frac{7}{8}$ (C) $\frac{11}{16}$ (D) $1\frac{5}{11}$

57. Which shows 0.45 as a reduced fraction?

   (A) 45   (B) $\frac{9}{20}$ (C) $\frac{9}{2}$ (D) $\frac{5}{100}$

58. Which shows 0.25 as a reduced fraction?

(A) 4   (B) $\dfrac{1}{4}$ (C) $\dfrac{25}{10}$ (D) none of these

59. Which shows 0.7 as a reduced fraction?

(A) $\dfrac{7}{10}$ (B) $\dfrac{1}{7}$ (C) $\dfrac{7}{1}$ (D) $\dfrac{7}{100}$

60. Write 0.49 as a fraction in simplest form.

Objective C: To identify the order of relation between two decimals or between a decimal and a fraction

Choose the correct symbol, >,<, or =.

61. 0.42 ___ 0.05

(A) >   (B) <   (C) =

62. $\dfrac{3}{8}$ ___ 0.37

(A) >   (B) <   (C) =

63. $\dfrac{17}{25}$ ___ 0.675

(A) >   (B) <   (C) =

64. 0.13 ___ $\dfrac{9}{20}$

(A) >   (B) <   (C) =

65. Insert the correct symbol, >,<, or = between the two numbers.

0.08 ___ $\dfrac{9}{20}$

Section 3.1 Introduction to Decimals

Objective A: To write decimals in standard form and in words

[1] (B)

[2] (A)

[3] (A)

[4] (C)

[5] four hundred thirty-three and sixty-one hundredths

Objective B: To round a decimal to a given place value

[6] (A)

[7] (B)

[8] (B)

[9] (A)

[10] 37.78

Section 3.2: Addition of Decimals

Objective A: To add decimals

[11] (B)

[12] (A)

[13] (D)

[14] (B)

[15] 498.4777

Objective B: To solve application problems

[16] (D)

[17] (A)

[18] (B)

[19] (A)

[20] $134.10

Section 3.3: Subtraction of Decimals

Objective A: To subtract decimals

[21] (B)

[22] (C)

[23] (D)

[24] (D)

[25] 528.41

Objective B: To solve application problems

[26] (A)

[27] (D)

[28] (C) _____

[29] (A) _____

[30] $1426.29 _____

Section 4.4: Multiplication of Decimals

Objective A: To multiply decimals

[31] (C) _____

[32] (A) _____

[33] (A) _____

[34] (D) _____

[35] 0.234546 _____

Objective B: To solve application problems

[36] (C) _____

[37] (A) _____

[38] (D) _____

[39] (A) _____

[40] $54.80 _____

Section 3.5: Division of Decimals

Objective A: To divide decimals

[41] (C)

[42] (A)

[43] (B)

[44] (A)

[45] 35

Objective B: To solve application problems

[46] (B)

[47] (A)

[48] (A)

[49] (D)

[50] $3.50

Section 3.6: Comparing and Converting Fractions and Decimals

Objective A: To convert fractions to decimals

[51] (C)

[52] (A)

[53] (D)

[54] (A) _____

[55] 0.04 _____

Objective B: To convert decimals to fractions

[56] (C) _____

[57] (B) _____

[58] (B) _____

[59] (A) _____

[60] $\dfrac{49}{100}$ _____

Objective C: To identify the order of relation between two decimals or between a decimal and a fraction

[61] (A) _____

[62] (A) _____

[63] (A) _____

[64] (B) _____

[65] $0.08 < \dfrac{9}{20}$ _____

Section 4.1: Ratio

Objective A: To write the ratio of two quantities in simplest form

Compare as a ratio in simplest form.

1. 9 cans to 4 bottles

    (A) $\dfrac{4}{9}$ (B) $\dfrac{9}{13}$ (C) $\dfrac{9}{4}$ (D) none of these

2. A history class consists of 15 males and 13 females.

    (A) $\dfrac{15}{13}$ (B) $\dfrac{13}{28}$ (C) $\dfrac{15}{28}$ (D) $\dfrac{13}{15}$

3. The male to female ratio in China is 52 to 48.

    (A) $\dfrac{13}{6}$ (B) $\dfrac{52}{48}$ (C) $\dfrac{13}{12}$ (D) $\dfrac{13}{24}$

4. The ratio of cars to people in Australia is 325 to 1000.

    (A) $\dfrac{13}{80}$ (B) $\dfrac{13}{20}$ (C) $\dfrac{325}{1000}$ (D) $\dfrac{13}{40}$

5. Compare as a ratio in simplest form using a fraction.
    In Iona's home town, the ratio of cars to people is 400 to 1000.

Objective B: To solve application problems

6. An astronaut who weighs 147 pounds on Earth would weigh 33 pounds on the
    Theta Space Station. If a piece of equipment weighed 1470 pounds on Earth, what would it weigh
    on the Theta Space Station?

    (A) 320 lb   (B) 380 lb   (C) 330 lb   (D) 363 lb

7. A worker on an assembly line takes 5 hours to produce 27 parts. At that rate, how many parts can
    she produce in 20 hours?

    (A) 108   (B) 6   (C) 540   (D) 216

8. The team's ratio of games won to games played was 5 to 9. If the team played 81 games, how many games did the team win?

    (A) 9   (B) 5   (C) 45   (D) 36

9. A map has a scale of 1 centimeter: 10 kilometers. If two cities are 11 centimeters apart on the map, what is the actual distance between the two cities?

    (A) 110 km   (B) 0.9 km   (C) 1100 km   (D) 1.1 km

10. A bus travels 90 miles on 6 gallons of gas. At that rate, how much gas will it need to travel 390 miles?

Section 4.2: Rates

Objective A: To write rates

Represent the ratio as a rate in lowest terms.

11. 110 calories for 90 crackers

    (A) $\dfrac{22 \text{ crackers}}{18 \text{ calories}}$ (B) $\dfrac{110 \text{ crackers}}{90 \text{ calories}}$ (C) $\dfrac{11 \text{ calories}}{9 \text{ crackers}}$ (D) $\dfrac{9 \text{ calories}}{11 \text{ crackers}}$

12. Patricia paid $588 for 6 nights at a hotel.

    (A) $\dfrac{\$588}{\text{night}}$ (B) $\dfrac{\$49}{\text{night}}$ (C) $\dfrac{\$196}{\text{night}}$ (D) $\dfrac{\$98}{\text{night}}$

13. $6.75 for 9 muffins

    (A) $\dfrac{\$0.70}{\text{muffin}}$ (B) $\dfrac{\$0.85}{\text{muffin}}$ (C) $\dfrac{\$0.75}{\text{muffin}}$ (D) $\dfrac{\$0.80}{\text{muffin}}$

14. $4.00 for 10 muffins

    (A) $\dfrac{\$0.35}{\text{muffin}}$ (B) $\dfrac{\$0.45}{\text{muffin}}$ (C) $\dfrac{\$0.30}{\text{muffin}}$ (D) $\dfrac{\$0.40}{\text{muffin}}$

15. 121 treats for 55 children

Objective B: To write unit rates

Express the ratio as a unit rate.

16. $2.40 for 15 ounces of popcorn

    (A) $1.60 per oz   (B) $0.36 per oz   (C) $0.60 per oz   (D) $0.16 per oz

17. 212 kilometers in 4 hours

    (A) 58 km per hr   (B) 48 km per hr   (C) 53 km per hr   (D) 63 km per hr

18. $24 in $\frac{1}{4}$ day

    (A) $96 per day   (B) $6 per day   (C) $48 per day   (D) $20 per day

19. A manufacturer can produce 1450 parts in 5 hours.

    (A) 290 parts per hour   (B) $\frac{1}{1160}$ part per hour

    (C) $\frac{1}{290}$ part per hour   (D) none of these

20. $47.25 for 35 disks

Objective C: To solve application problems

21. A cyclist can travel 36.9 miles in 3 hours. How far can the same cyclist travel in 7 hours?

    (A) 88.1 mi   (B) 85.5 mi   (C) 86.1 mi   (D) none of these

22. Tina reads 14 pages every day. At that rate, how many pages will she read in 1 week?

    (A) 98   (B) 108   (C) 88   (D) 96

23. An architect drew 22 plans in 5 months. How many plans could the architect draw in 35 months?

    (A) 110   (B) 157   (C) 154   (D) 155

24. Tom is buying a package of crayons at a store. The store sells packages of 7 crayons for $0.77 and 11 crayons for $1.98. Which package offers the better unit price?

    (A) 7 crayons for $0.77

    (B) 11 crayons for $1.98

    (C) both offer the same unit price

    (D) not enough information to tell

25. Thomas is buying a package of gum balls at a store. The store sells packages of 6 gum balls for $0.72 and 13 gum balls for $2.21. Which package offers the better unit price?

Section 4.3: Proportions

Objective A: To determine whether a proportion is true

26. Which of the following pairs of ratios is not a true proportion?

    (A) $\dfrac{4}{5} = \dfrac{16}{25}$ (B) $\dfrac{4}{5} = \dfrac{12}{15}$ (C) $\dfrac{4}{5} = \dfrac{40}{50}$ (D) $\dfrac{4}{5} = \dfrac{16}{20}$

27. Which of the following pairs of ratios is a true proportion?

    (A) $\dfrac{3}{8} = \dfrac{15}{24}$ (B) $\dfrac{3}{8} = \dfrac{12}{16}$ (C) $\dfrac{3}{8} = \dfrac{9}{24}$ (D) $\dfrac{3}{8} = \dfrac{6}{40}$

28. Which of the following pairs of ratios is *not* a true proportion?

    (A) $\dfrac{3}{8} = \dfrac{9}{24}$ (B) $\dfrac{3}{8} = \dfrac{12}{32}$ (C) $\dfrac{3}{8} = \dfrac{9}{32}$ (D) $\dfrac{27}{72} = \dfrac{3}{8}$

29. Which of the following pairs of ratios is a true proportion?

    (A) $\dfrac{7}{6} = \dfrac{35}{30}$ (B) $\dfrac{35}{6} = \dfrac{7}{30}$ (C) $\dfrac{8}{6} = \dfrac{35}{30}$ (D) $\dfrac{7}{6} = \dfrac{36}{30}$

30. Is the following pair of ratios a true proportion?
    $$\dfrac{2}{7} = \dfrac{16}{56}$$

Objective B: To solve proportions

Solve.

31. $\dfrac{2}{5} = \dfrac{8}{x}$

   (A) 8   (B) 20   (C) 34   (D) 27

32. $\dfrac{j}{2} = \dfrac{3}{12}$

   (A) $\dfrac{1}{6}$ (B) $\dfrac{1}{2}$ (C) $\dfrac{1}{4}$ (D) none of these

33. $\dfrac{2}{8} = \dfrac{x}{24}$

   (A) 5   (B) 9   (C) 6   (D) 11

34. $\dfrac{3}{4} = \dfrac{a}{92}$

   (A) 69   (B) 12   (C) 23   (D) 67

35. $\dfrac{x}{8} = \dfrac{21}{24}$

Objective C: To solve application problems

36. If 3 tins of pears cost $2.07, how many tins of pears can you buy for $8.97?

   (A) 14   (B) 3   (C) 39   (D) 13

37. Chen is making an appetizer for an upcoming party and needs beans to complete the recipe. He has $10.36 to spend. If 2 cans of beans cost $1.48, how many cans of beans can he buy?

   (A) 28   (B) 15   (C) 14   (D) 5

38. A wholesale flower shop is advertising 2 bunches of flowers for $1.48. If a customer spends $6.66 at the shop, how many bunches of flowers did the customer buy?

   (A) 8   (B) 18   (C) 3   (D) 9

39. Geothermal energy is heat from inside the earth. Underground temperatures generally increase 9°C for every 300 meters of depth. How deep would a well have to be for the temperature to be 198°C greater than the surface temperature?

(A) 13.6 m   (B) 660 m   (C) 66 m   (D) 6600 m

40. Mr. Jones took a survey of college students and found that 40 out of 48 students are liberal arts majors. If a college has 11,631 students, what is the expected number of students who are liberal arts majors?

Chapter 4 Ratio and Proportion

Section 4.1: Ratio

Objective A: To write the ratio of two quantities in simplest form

[1] (C)

[2] (A)

[3] (C)

[4] (D)

[5] $\dfrac{2}{5}$

Objective B: To solve application problems

[6] (C)

[7] (A)

[8] (C)

[9] (A)

[10] 26 gal

Section 4.2: Rates

Objective A: To write rates

[11] (C)

[12] (D)

[13] <u>(C)</u>

[14] <u>(D)</u>

[15] $\dfrac{11 \text{ treats}}{5 \text{ children}}$

Objective B: To write unit rates

[16] <u>(D)</u>

[17] <u>(C)</u>

[18] <u>(A)</u>

[19] <u>(A)</u>

[20] $1.35 per disk

Objective C: To solve application problems

[21] <u>(C)</u>

[22] <u>(A)</u>

[23] <u>(C)</u>

[24] <u>(A)</u>

[25] 6 gum balls for $0.72

Section 4.3: Proportions

Objective A: To determine whether a proportion is true

[26] <u>(A)</u>

[27] (C)

[28] (C)

[29] (A)

[30] Yes

Objective B: To solve proportions

[31] (B)

[32] (B)

[33] (C)

[34] (A)

[35] 7

Objective C: To solve application problems

[36] (D)

[37] (C)

[38] (D)

[39] (D)

[40] 9693

Chapter 5 Percents

Section 5.1: Intro to Percents

Objective A: To write a percent as a fraction or decimal

1. Which shows 6% as a decimal?

   (A) 0.6   (B) 0.06   (C) 0.0006   (D) 0.006

2. Which shows 1.3% as a decimal?

   (A) 0.0013   (B) 0.00013   (C) 0.013   (D) 0.13

3. Which shows 20% as a reduced fraction?

   (A) $\frac{9}{50}$ (B) $\frac{11}{50}$ (C) $\frac{20}{100}$ (D) $\frac{1}{5}$

4. Which shows 66% as a reduced fraction?

   (A) $\frac{33}{50}$ (B) $\frac{33}{5}$ (C) $\frac{33}{25}$ (D) $\frac{66}{25}$

5. Write 1% as a reduced fraction.

Objective B: To write a fraction or decimal as a percent

6. Which shows $\frac{1}{2}$ as a percent?

   (A) 0.2%   (B) 0.5%   (C) 2%   (D) 50%

7. Which shows $\frac{3}{8}$ as a percent?

   (A) 26.6667%   (B) 0.375%   (C) 38%   (D) 37.5%

8. Which shows $\frac{7}{10}$ as a percent?

   (A) 70%   (B) 66%   (C) 68%   (D) 72%

9. Which shows $\frac{1}{5}$ as a percent?

   (A) 0.5% (B) 0.2% (C) 5% (D) 20%

10. Write $\frac{3}{5}$ as a percent.

Section 5.2: Percent Equations Part 1

Objective A: To find the amount when the percent and the base are given

11. Which is $66\frac{2}{3}$% of 66?

   (A) 44 (B) 22 (C) 11 (D) 33

12. Which is $50\frac{1}{2}$% of 30?

   (A) 15.15 (B) 151.5 (C) 0.06 (D) 1.515

13. Which is 50% of 12?

   (A) 0.6 (B) 11 (C) $\frac{50}{12}$ (D) none of these

14. Which is 63% of 59?

   (A) 37.17 (B) 35.17 (C) 2.07 (D) 1.07

15. What is $33\frac{1}{3}$% of 6?

Objective B: To solve application problems

16. Tom wants to buy a used car and needs to have a down payment of 20%. If the car Tom wants to buy costs $4200, how much down payment will he need?

   (A) $840 (B) $2000 (C) $3360 (D) $2200

17. Which is the salesperson's commission on a $600 sale if the commission rate is 10%?

   (A) $60   (B) $6000   (C) $606   (D) $6

18. Cecile wants to buy a bicycle that costs $202.00. Her parents say Cecile must raise 50% of the money herself. How much money must Cecile raise?

   (A) $98   (B) $153   (C) $101   (D) $151

19. Michael's softball team won 55% of the 67 games it played. How many games did it win?

   (A) 34   (B) 37   (C) 30   (D) 40

20. Tom wants to buy a used car and needs to have a down payment of 35%. If the car Tom wants to buy costs $6200, how much down payment will he need?

Section 5.3: Percent Equations Part 2

Objective A: To find the percent when the base and amount are given

21. Which percent of 1900 is 95?

   (A) 180,499%   (B) 5%   (C) 180,500%   (D) 20%

22. Which percent of 4 is 640?

   (A) 0.0000625%   (B) 16,000%   (C) 160%   (D) none of these

23. Which percent of 16 is 8?

   (A) 50%   (B) 2%   (C) $\frac{1}{2}$%   (D) 0.5%

24. Which percent of 8 is 40?

   (A) 500%   (B) 0.002%   (C) 20%   (D) none of these

25. What percent of 1800 is 90?

Objective B: To solve application problems

26. Vanessa made 15 of 20 free throws at basketball practice. Which percent did she make?

   (A) 5%   (B) 75%   (C) 25%   (D) 42.9%

27. A paint store gives a discount to 5 of every 10 customers. Which percent of the customers receives a discount?

(A) 5% (B) 0.05% (C) $\frac{1}{2}$% (D) 50%

28. Of every 8 chocolate bars Russell sold, 5 had almonds. Which percent had almonds?

(A) 6.25% (B) 0.625% (C) 62.5% (D) $\frac{5}{8}$%

29. Murray correctly answered 54 questions on a 60 question social studies test. Which percent did Murray get correct?

(A) 62% (B) 70% (C) 65% (D) 90%

30. Last month the Rams played the Dolphins 5 times and defeated them 2 times. What percent of the games did the Rams lose?

Section 5.4: Percent Equations Part 3

Objective A: To find the base when the percent and amount are given

31. 24 is $66\frac{2}{3}$% of which number?

(A) 0.16 (B) 800 (C) 36 (D) none of these

32. 320 is 400% of which number?

(A) 128,000 (B) 2000 (C) 82 (D) none of these

33. 12 is 80% of which number?

(A) 150 (B) $\frac{12}{80}$ (C) 15 (D) none of these

34. 150 is 60% of which number?

(A) 250 (B) 2500 (C) 9 (D) 90

35. 625.4 is 265% of what number?

Objective B: To solve application problems

36. A ski club planned a trip to Squaw Valley and 7 of the members signed up to go. If this is 10% of the total membership, how many members are in the ski club?

    (A) 700   (B) 7   (C) 1   (D) 70

37. During the soccer season, Cathy scored goals on 11% of the shots she took. If she scored 77 goals, how many shots did she take?

    (A) 85   (B) 70   (C) 847   (D) 700

38. Margarette correctly answered 60 questions on a English test. She received a score of 75%. How many questions were on the test?

    (A) 80   (B) 105   (C) 77   (D) 107

39. Jeff is a salesperson in a retail store and earns $56 per week plus 8% of his weekly sales. If Jeff earned $648 one week, what were his sales that week?

    (A) $51.84   (B) $7400.00   (C) $8800.00   (D) $47.36

40. During the volleyball season Lorin scored on 17% of the spikes she took. If she scored 51 spikes, how many spikes did she take?

Section 5.5: Percent Problems: Proportion Method

Objective A: To solve percent problems using proportions

Solve.

41. Which is 70% of 80?

    (A) 56%   (B) 15   (C) $\dfrac{7}{8}$ (D) 56

42. Which is 20% of 40?

    (A) 8   (B) $\dfrac{1}{2}$ (C) 80   (D) 8%

43. Which is 25% of 108?

    (A) 27   (B) 270   (C) 260   (D) 26

Solve.

44. Which is 5.4% of 300?

   (A) 16.2   (B) 1620   (C) 55.5556   (D) 1.8

45. 6.2% of 600 is what number?

Objective B: To solve application problems

46. Mario bought a pair of shoes priced at $20.00. If the sales tax rate in Mario's state is 8%, which is the total price of the shoes?

   (A) $16.00   (B) $1.60   (C) $21.60   (D) none of these

47. A drapery regularly selling for $35.99 is advertised at 55% off. Which is the sale price?

   (A) $16.20   (B) $34.01   (C) $19.79   (D) $55.78

48. A store buys blouses for $15 each and marks them up by 60% for retail sale. Which is the retail price of each of the blouses?

   (A) $15.90   (B) $17.00   (C) $150.00   (D) $24.00

49. A coffee table regularly sells for $224. The coffee table is currently on sale at a 30% discount. If the sales tax is 7.35%, which is the total cost of the coffee table?

   (A) $11.52   (B) $16.46   (C) $240.46   (D) $168.32

50. Chuck bought a pair of boots priced at $31.00. If the sales tax rate in Chuck's state is 4%, what is the sales tax on the boots?

Chapter 5 Percents

Section 5.1: Intro to Percents

Objective A: To write a percent as a fraction or decimal

[1] (B) _____

[2] (C) _____

[3] (D) _____

[4] (A) _____

[5] $\dfrac{1}{100}$ _____

Objective B: To write a fraction or decimal as a percent

[6] (D) _____

[7] (D) _____

[8] (A) _____

[9] (D) _____

[10] 60% _____

Section 5.2: Percent Equations Part 1

Objective A: To find the amount when the percent and the base are given

[11] (A) _____

[12] (A) _____

[13] (D) _____

[14] (A)

[15] 2

Objective B: To solve application problems

[16] (A)

[17] (A)

[18] (C)

[19] (B)

[20] $2170

Section 5.3: Percent Equations Part 2

Objective A: To find the percent when the base and amount are given

[21] (B)

[22] (B)

[23] (A)

[24] (A)

[25] 5%

Objective B: To solve application problems

[26] (B)

[27] (D)

[28] (C)

[29] (D)

[30] 60%

Section 5.4: Percent Equations Part 3

Objective A: To find the base when the percent and amount are given

[31] (C)

[32] (D)

[33] (C)

[34] (A)

[35] 236

Objective B: To solve application problems

[36] (D)

[37] (D)

[38] (A)

[39] (B)

[40] 300

Section 5.5: Percent Problems: Proportion Method

Objective A: To solve percent problems using proportions

[41] (D)

[42] (A)

[43] (A)

[44] (A)

[45] 37.2

Objective B: To solve application problems

[46] (C)

[47] (A)

[48] (D)

[49] (D)

[50] $1.24

Chapter 6 Applications for Business and Consumers

Section 6.1: Applications to Purchasing

Objective A: To find unit cost

1. A 3-kilogram box of laundry soap costs $4.11. Which is the cost per kilogram?

   (A) $1.27   (B) $7.11   (C) $1.37   (D) $4.37

2. Andrew spent $2.87 at the stationery store. If he bought 7 note pads, how much did each note pad cost?

   (A) $0.41   (B) $0.40   (C) $20.09   (D) $0.39

3. Dina borrowed $1854.00 to buy a computer. She wants to pay back the loan with 9 equal payments. Which will be the amount of each payment?

   (A) $215.00   (B) $206.00   (C) $197.00   (D) $214.00

4. The cost of decorations and refreshments for a party given by 5 friends was $120. If each person shared the cost equally, how much did each person pay?

   (A) $6   (B) $30   (C) $26   (D) $24

5. Kristy borrowed $2133.00 from her grandmother to buy a used car. She wants to pay back her grandmother with 9 equal payments. What will be the amount of each payment?

Objective B: To find the most economical purchase

6. Which is the best buy?

   (A) 14 bars of soap for $13.86   (B) 8 bars of soap for $8.00

   (C) 7 bars of soap for $7.14   (D) 10 bars of soap for $9.70

7. Which is the best buy?

   (A) $40.60 for 14 bars of soap   (B) $20.09 for 7 bars of soap

   (C) $42.90 for 15 bars of soap   (D) $25.65 for 9 bars of soap

8. Which is the best buy?

   (A) 11 burritos for $7.92   (B) 5 burritos for $3.55

   (C) 6 burritos for $4.08   (D) 12 burritos for $8.76

9. Which is the best buy?

   (A) 6 cookies for $3.42

   (C) 9 cookies for $4.86

   (B) 8 cookies for $4.40

   (D) 14 cookies for $7.28

10. For a science project, Rachel needs some tubes. She spends $4 on 4 plastic tubes, and $10 on 2 metal tubes. How much more is the unit cost of a metal tube than the unit cost of a plastic tube?

Objective C: To find total cost

11. The local butcher shop sells prime rib at $4.39 per pound. What would it cost to purchase 9 pounds of prime rib at this butcher shop?

    (A) $13.39   (B) $39.51   (C) $63.22   (D) $34.81

12. A roadside fruit stand sells pears at $0.34 apiece. Which is the total cost for 10 pears?

    (A) $18.61   (B) $3.40   (C) $10.34   (D) $4.76

13. A designer perfume sells for $0.50 per milliliter. Find the total cost to buy 6.1 milliliters of the perfume.

    (A) $6.60   (B) $2.55   (C) $3.05   (D) $2.14

14. Imported bananas cost $1.78 per pound. How how much would it cost to buy 3.6 pounds of bananas?

    (A) $5.38   (B) $6.41   (C) $8.97   (D) $2.02

15. If an expensive mint candy costs $7.39 per pound, find the cost to purchase $\frac{3}{4}$ pound of the candy. Round your answer to the nearest cent.

Section 6.2: Percent Increase and Percent Decrease

Objective A: To find percent increase

16. The figure below shows the balance in a savings account from April through June. Which is the percent of decrease from May to June?

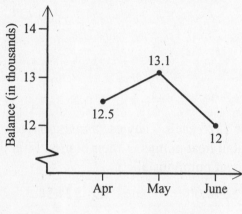

    (A) 9.2%   (B) 4.8%   (C) 8.4%   (D) 4.6%

17. A clothing consignment store purchased a coat for $23.12 and then sold it for $26.61. Find the percent of increase.

    (A) 15.1%   (B) 115.1%   (C) 86.9%   (D) 13.1%

18. In 2001, the circulation of a local newspaper increased from 6928 papers sold in January to 11,099 papers sold in December. Find the percent of increase.

    (A) 60.2%   (B) 62.4%   (C) 160.2%   (D) 37.6%

19. The graph shows the amount reported in sales for a software company over a four year period. Find the percent of decrease in sales from 1995 to 1996.

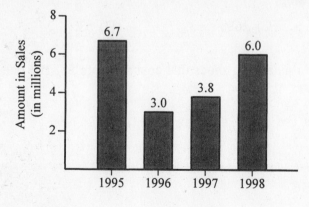

    (A) 223.3%   (B) 44.8%   (C) 123.3%   (D) 55.2%

20. The table shows the revenue of a local automobile dealership. Find the percent of decrease in the revenue from 1996 to 1998. Round to the nearest tenth of a percent.

Year	Revenue
1992	125,000
1996	135,000
1998	115,000
2001	325,000

Objective B: To apply percent increase to business - markup

21. ComforTemp purchases heat pumps from a supplier for $325 each. They use a markup rate of 15% to set the price that they will charge homeowners to install heat pumps in their homes. Find the markup that a homeowner must pay in order to have a heat pump installed.

    (A) $48.75   (B) $487.50   (C) $340.00   (D) $24.38

22. SuperQuip added 270 adult-sized shoulder pads to its inventory in preparation for the upcoming football season. If each of the shoulder pads cost SuperQuip $40 and the markup rate is 30%, which is the markup per shoulder pad?

    (A) $60.00   (B) $12.00   (C) $70.00   (D) $18.00

23. A struggling furniture store owner determines that in order to make a profit, she must set a 44% markup rate for every item in her store. Find the markup on a sofa that cost the owner $100 to stock.

    (A) $36.00   (B) $44.00   (C) $60.00   (D) $70.40

24. Cycle Stop Bike Sales is offering a markup of $215 on a new bicycle that cost them $820 to stock. Find the markup rate for this bicycle at Cycle Stop.

    (A) 38%   (B) 6%   (C) 26%   (D) 53%

25. In-Step Dancing Supplies uses a markup of $7 on dancing shoes that cost the store $38 per pair. What is percent of markup for the shoes?

Objective C: To find percent decrease

26. A chef discovered a new method for roasting leg of lamb that reduced the cooking time by 34 minutes. What percent decrease in time does this represent if it used to take him 155 minutes for the same task?

   (A) 73%   (B) 22%   (C) 121%   (D) 20%

27. An upgrade in insulation materials led to a $310 reduction in the monthly power bill at Really Cold Storage, Inc. If the monthly power bill was $1140 before the upgrade, what percent decrease does the reduction in the bill represent?

   (A) 1450%   (B) 830%   (C) 27%   (D) 41%

28. A used appliance store estimates that the value of an oven-range combination decreases by 30% in the first year of use. If the original price of a one-year-old oven-range combination was $1250, how much value will this store probably say the appliance lost?

   (A) $375.00   (B) $41.67   (C) $1220.00   (D) $188.00

29. A large farm employs seasonal workers to help harvest its crop. During the harvesting season, the farm has 1470 employees. At the end of the harvesting season, the farm releases 45% of its employees. Which is the decrease in the number of employees?

   (A) 661.5   (B) 66,150   (C) 1020   (D) 331

30. A decrease in demand led a small computer chip manufacturing plant to reduce its production of microprocessor cooling fans from 2800 per month to 802 per month.
   a. What is the amount of decrease in microprocessor fans produced?
   b. What percent decrease in microprocessor fan production is represented by this amount?

Objective D: To apply percent decrease to business - discount

31. A local music store is offering a discount of $58 on guitar cases. If guitar cases usually sell for $87 at this store, find the discount rate.

   (A) $29\frac{1}{3}$%   (B) $15\frac{2}{3}$%   (C) $5\frac{1}{3}$%   (D) $66\frac{2}{3}$%

32. A Used Tire store is selling minimally-worn tires for $52 off the new-tire-price of $78 each. Find the discount rate on these tires.

   (A) $66\frac{2}{3}$%   (B) $5\frac{1}{3}$%   (C) $15\frac{2}{3}$%   (D) $26\frac{1}{3}$%

33. Quicksell Computers, Inc. is selling flat-panel computer monitors for 10% off the regular price of $330. Find the discount.

    (A) $13   (B) $320   (C) $33   (D) $10

34. Theatre Outfitters International is advertising full-size movie screens for 25% off the regular price. If the regular price of a full-size screen is $456, find the discount.

    (A) $431   (B) $114   (C) $68   (D) $25

35. Jessica received a $49 discount on a trampoline she bought for backyard exercise. If the regular price of the trampoline was $245, find the discount rate that Jessica received on the trampoline.

Section 6.3: Interest

Objective A: To calculate simple interest

36. Michael put $5000 in a savings account. At the end of 2 years the account had earned $700 in interest. Which annual simple interest rate did the account earn?

    (A) 13.5%   (B) 6.0%   (C) 14.5%   (D) 7.0%

37. How much interest will Bill pay on his car loan if he finances $12,000 at a 10% simple interest rate for 3 years?

    (A) $400   (B) $360   (C) $1200   (D) $3600

38. Sylvia bought a 6-month $1100 certificate of deposit. At the end of 6 months, she received $88 simple interest. Which rate of interest did the certificate pay?

    (A) 13.3%   (B) 16%   (C) 8%   (D) 32%

39. Sally bought a 6-month $900 certificate of deposit. At the end of 6 months, she received $36 simple interest. Which annual rate of interest did the certificate pay?

    (A) 16%   (B) 4%   (C) 8%   (D) 6.7%

40. A savings account is set up so that the simple interest earned on the investment is moved into a separate checking account at the end of each year. If $7000 is invested at 4.5%, what is the total simple interest accumulated in the checking account after 4 years?

Objective B: To calculate finance charges on a credit card bill

41. Jan's credit card charges 1.5% on the monthly unpaid balance on the card. If her unpaid balance is $199.24, find the finance charge.

  (A) $2.99   (B) $132.83   (C) $1.50   (D) $4.19

42. Fred used a store credit card to make a large purchase during a store promotion that offered 3 months of interest-free credit. After the 3 months, the finance charge on unpaid monthly balances would be 4.5%. If his purchase was for $545.07 and Fred made 3 monthly payments of $136.27 afterward, find the finance charge on the unpaid balance at the end of the fourth month?

  (A) $18.40   (B) $98.08   (C) $6.13   (D) $24.53

43. A credit card company has a finance charge of 1% per month for any unpaid balances. What is the finance charge for an unpaid balance of $12,023.94?

  (A) $192.38   (B) $36.07   (C) $120.24   (D) $12,023.94

44. Your credit card company informs you that they are reducing the rate that you must pay on unpaid credit card balances to 2.2%. How much will you pay on the next bill for an unpaid balance of $1065.55?

  (A) $23.44   (B) $14.06   (C) $484.34   (D) $35.16

45. Juanita and Harris have identical unpaid balances of $1695.47 on their credit cards. Juanita's card charges 2.4% on unpaid balances while Harris's card charges 2%. What is the difference in the amounts that they will pay for finance charges?

Objective C: To calculate compound interest

46. The following table shows the balance of a bank account at the end of each year for four years. If $310.00 is initially invested, and the interest is compounded annually, which is the interest rate for the account?

Years in Account	Balance
0	$310.00
1	$320.08
2	$330.48
3	$341.22
4	$352.31

  (A) 1.9%   (B) 2%   (C) 3.25%   (D) 3.15%

47. If a principal of $1080 is invested at an annual interest rate of 5% compounded annually, which is the account balance at the end of 6 years?

(A) $1447   (B) $1378   (C) $1404   (D) $6804

48. An amount of $340 is invested at an annual interest rate of 4.25% compounded annually. The following table shows the balance of the account at the end of each year. Complete the table to determine the balance in the account at the end of 6 years.

Year	Balance
0	$340.00
1	$354.45
2	$369.51
3	
4	
5	
6	

(A) $436.45   (B) $467.55   (C) $502.30   (D) $379.04

49. If $1480 is invested in an account which earns 7% interest compounded annually, which will be the balance of the account at the end of 14 years?

(A) $2,491,992   (B) $2930   (C) $22,170   (D) $3816

50. If a principal of $1430 is invested at an annual interest rate of 4% compounded annually, what is the account balance at the end of 4 years?

Section 6.4: Real Estate Expenses

Objective A: To calculate the initial expenses of buying a home

51. Steven purchased an espresso stand for $40,000. The lender required a down payment of 20% of the purchase price. Find the down payment.

(A) $3800   (B) $38,000   (C) $800   (D) $8000

52. Maria purchased a new duplex rental home for $105,500. A down payment of 30% of the purchase price was required by the lender. Find the down payment.

(A) $3165   (B) $102,500   (C) $31,650   (D) $10,250

53. Zachary made a down payment that was 15% of the purchase price on a graphics design company priced at $800,000. How much was the down payment?

(A) $12,000   (B) $120,000   (C) $200,000   (D) $20,000

54. A condominium sold for $180,000, and a down payment of 25% of the purchase price was made at closing. Find the down payment made on the condominium.

(A) $4500   (B) $27,000   (C) $45,000   (D) $270,000

55. A local construction company is selling retail space in a new mall for $390,000. A down payment of 10% of the purchase price is required. Find the down payment.

Objective B: To calculate ongoing expenses of owning a home

56. Top Rate Savings and Loan, Inc. requires a down payment of 15% of the purchase price on an oceanfront home priced at $675,000. Find the down payment and the remaining mortgage on the home.

(A) $1,012,500; $337,500   (B) $67,350; $607,650

(C) $101,250; $573,750   (D) $673,500; $1500

57. Brianna purchased a horse stable for $510,000. The bank requires a down payment of 10% of the purchase price. Find the down payment and the remaining mortgage on the stable.

(A) $102,000; $408,000   (B) $1,020,000; $510,000

(C) $10,200; $499,800   (D) $51,000; $459,000

58. A local hardware store purchased some land for $205,000. The bank required a 15% down payment on the purchase price of the land. Find the down payment and the remaining mortgage on the land.

(A) $30,750; $174,250   (B) $307,500; $102,500

(C) $41,000; $164,000   (D) $410,000; $205,000

59. Seth purchased a condominium at Lake Murray. The lender required a down payment of 15% on the condominium's purchase price. Find Seth's remaining mortgage if the original purchase price was $255,000.

(A) $252,450   (B) $216,750   (C) $127,500   (D) $229,500

60. A bank requires a down payment of 5% of the purchase price of a home for all customers qualifying for their first-time buyers program. Find the remaining mortgage required for a first-time buyer when the purchase price of a home is $160,000.

Section 6.5: Car Expenses

Objective A: To calculate the initial expenses of buying a car

61. Jade plans on purchasing a new SUV that costs $23,500. The dealer requires a down payment of 15% of the purchase price. Can Jade make the down payment if she has saved $5405 toward the purchase of the SUV? If not, determine how much more money Jade should raise in order to make the down payment?

    (A) No; $940   (B) Yes   (C) No; $1057   (D) No; $235

62. Anna made a 14% down payment on a sports car priced at $16,344. Find the amount of the down payment.

    (A) $11,440.80   (B) $22,881.60   (C) $1144.08   (D) $2288.16

63. A local construction company bought a one-ton truck to carry tools and supplies. The company paid a 6.5% sales tax on the purchase price of the truck. Find the sales tax if the truck sold for $30,000.

    (A) $195.00   (B) $390.00   (C) $1950.00   (D) $3900.00

64. Brandon purchased a used sedan for $6738. He paid a sales tax of 7% on the purchase price of the car. Find the sales tax.

    (A) $943.32   (B) $2358.30   (C) $471.66   (D) $47.17

65. Isabella was charged a licensing fee of 3.5% of the purchase price paid for a $8200 car. Find the licensing fee on the car.

Objective B: To calculate ongoing expenses of owning a car

66. A credit union finances a truck loan of $10,270 for 5 years at an annual interest rate of 7%. Find the monthly truck payment.

    (A) $203.36   (B) $731.52   (C) $345.71   (D) $68.05

67. An estimate for parts and service for an RV is $.055 per mile. Use this estimate to determine the projected costs for parts and service during a vacation in which the RV will be driven 11,560 miles.

(A) $8901.20 (B) $890.12 (C) $635.80 (D) $6358.00

68. An independent contractor spent $989 on maintenance during a year in which he drove his car 18,041 miles. Find the cost per mile for maintenance on the car.

(A) $0.055 (B) $0.01 (C) $0.088 (D) $0.006

69. Last year Lance drove his car 13,935 miles and spent $370 on repairs. Find Lance's cost per mile for repairs on his car.

(A) $0.035 (B) $0.027 (C) $0.003 (D) $0.004

70. Abigail purchased a camper for $19,200 and made a down payment of $2880. The balance is financed for 6 years at an annual interest rate of 8%. Find the amount financed and the monthly payment for the camper.

Section 6.6: Wages

Objective A: To calculate commissions, total hourly wages, and salaries

71. Taylor is a lifeguard at a public swimming pool. He earns an hourly wage of $8.00. How much will Taylor earn for working 18 hours?

(A) $144.00 (B) $152.00 (C) $14.40 (D) $225.00

72. Garrett works part-time for a clothing store and receives a commission of 39% on his weekly sales. Find Garrett's commission for sales of $1208.

(A) $39.00 (B) $47.11 (C) $309.74 (D) $471.12

73. Sales representatives at a car dealership earn a commission of 18% for cars sold. Find the commission earned on a sedan purchased for $15,541.

(A) $86.34 (B) $27,973.80 (C) $2797.38 (D) $863.39

74. An editor's hourly wage is $17.25. If she earns one and a half times her hourly wage for overtime, find her hourly wage when working overtime.

(A) $3.45 (B) $2.59 (C) $34.50 (D) $25.88

75. A marketing agent for a publishing company ears a 17% commission on magazine sales. Find the commission earned on magazine sales of $1685.

Section 6.7: Bank Statements

Objective A: To calculate checkbook balances

76. Sophie made a deposit of $626.31 in her money market account. Her original balance was $9641.61. Find the account balance after the deposit.

   (A) $10,267.92   (B) $10,355.75   (C) $9032.78   (D) $9015.30

77. Alberto had $643.71 in his savings account and made a withdrawal of $115.36. Find the new savings account balance.

   (A) $780.44   (B) $466.52   (C) $528.35   (D) $759.07

78. A gift shop had a balance of $5130.13 in its checking account. Find the account balance after a check for $2422.76 is written.

   (A) $2705.24   (B) $7552.89   (C) $7548.57   (D) $2707.37

79. A financial manager showed a balance of $9214.22 in the company checkbook. Find the balance in the checkbook after a deposit of $6650.52.

   (A) $2563.70   (B) $15,869.13   (C) $15,864.74   (D) $2557.94

80. Terence had a checkbook balance of $1436.08. He wrote a check for $262.22 and then made a deposit of $38.58. What is the current checkbook balance?

Objective B: To balance a checkbook

81. Balance the checkbook. Which accurately describes the relationship between the checkbook registry and the bank statement?

		RECORD ALL CHARGES OR CREDITS THAT AFFECT YOUR ACCOUNT							
NUMBER	DATE	DESCRIPTION OF TRANSACTION	PAYMENT/DEBIT (−)	T	FEE (IF ANY) (−)	DEPOSIT/CREDIT (+)		BALANCE	
								1300	95
516	7/6	Rent	423 74	✓				877	21
517	7/6	Water	80 99	✓				796	22
518	7/7	Electricity	40 94	✓				755	27
	7/10	Deposit		✓		828	33	1583	61
	7/15	Cash	25 00	✓				1558	61
519	7/23	Car	468 75					1089	86
	7/24	Deposit		✓		885	71	1975	57
	7/29	Interest		✓		59	27	2034	84

CHECKING ACCOUNT Monthly Statement		Account Number: 714 - 407 - 3	
Date	Transaction	Amount	Balance
7/5	OPENING BALANCE		1300.95
7/8	CHECK	413.74	887.21
7/8	CHECK	80.99	806.22
7/10	DEPOSIT	828.33	1634.55
7/15	WITHDRAWAL	25.00	1609.55
7/15	CHECK	40.94	1568.61
7/24	DEPOSIT	885.71	2454.32
7/29	INTEREST	59.27	2513.59
8/5	CLOSING BALANCE		2513.59

(A) The checkbook does not balance. An incorrect deposit entry occurred on 7/10.

(B) The checkbook does not balance. The entry for check 516 is incorrect.

(C) The checkbook does not balance. The entry for check 518 is incorrect.

(D) The bank statement and the checkbook balance.

82. Balance the checkbook. Which value, when entered into the checkbook registry for check 2164, will allow the checkbook and bank statement to balance?

		RECORD ALL CHARGES OR CREDITS THAT AFFECT YOUR ACCOUNT					BALANCE	
NUMBER	DATE	DESCRIPTION OF TRANSACTION	PAYMENT/DEBIT (–)	√T	FEE (IF ANY) (–)	DEPOSIT/CREDIT (+)	749	21
2162	10/15	Phone	25 69	✓			723	52
	10/16	Deposit		✓		842 33	1565	85
	10/18	Student Loan	275 00	✓			1290	85
	10/23	Fee		✓	3.00		1287	85
2163	10/25	Clothing	125 87	✓			1161	98
	10/29	Interest		✓		40 67	1202	65
2164	10/30	Credit Card					765	40

CHECKING ACCOUNT Monthly Statement		Account Number: 822-333-5	
Date	Transaction	Amount	Balance
10/5	OPENING BALANCE		749.21
10/16	DEPOSIT	842.33	723.52
10/17	CHECK	25.69	1565.85
10/20	CHECK	275.00	1290.85
10/23	FEE	3.00	1287.85
10/28	CHECK	125.87	1161.98
10/29	INTEREST	40.67	1202.65
11/5	CLOSING BALANCE		1202.65

(A) $435.72   (B) $43.73   (C) $437.25   (D) $447.25

83. Balance the checkbook. What dollar amount should be placed into the empty "Payment/Debit" entry for check number 3197 to ensure the checkbook balances appropriately?

		RECORD ALL CHARGES OR CREDITS THAT AFFECT YOUR ACCOUNT							
NUMBER	DATE	DESCRIPTION OF TRANSACTION	PAYMENT/DEBIT (–)		T	FEE (IF ANY) (–)	DEPOSIT/CREDIT (+)		BALANCE
									1287 96
3195	6/19	Car Pmt	458	62	✓				829 34
3196	6/20	Gas	109	71	✓				719 63
3197	6/20	Insurance							
	6/22	Deposit			✓		850	25	
3198	6/26	Rent	755	95	✓				
3199	6/28	Groceries	108	22	✓				
	6/30	Interest			✓		19	38	

CHECKING ACCOUNT Monthly Statement			Account Number: 678-467-5	
Date	Transaction		Amount	Balance
6/18	OPENING BALANCE			1287.96
6/22	CHECK		458.62	829.34
6/22	CHECK		109.71	719.63
6/22	DEPOSIT		850.25	498.52
6/23	CHECK		221.11	1348.77
6/29	CHECK		755.95	592.82
6/29	CHECK		108.22	484.60
6/30	INTEREST		19.38	503.98
6/30	CLOSING BALANCE			503.98

(A) $221.11   (B) $241.11   (C) $219.38   (D) $22.11

84. An error occurred on your monthly checking account statement from the bank. Complete the right-hand column to find the closing balance for the bank statement. What is the correct closing balance?

RECORD ALL CHARGES OR CREDITS THAT AFFECT YOUR ACCOUNT								
NUMBER	DATE	DESCRIPTION OF TRANSACTION	PAYMENT/DEBIT (–)	√T	FEE (IF ANY) (–)	DEPOSIT/CREDIT (+)	BALANCE	
							1522	07
421	6/1	Groceries	91 95	√			1430	12
422	6/2	Rent	465 75	√			964	37
	6/4	Deposit		√		700 80	1665	17
423	6/6	Credit Card	375 89	√			1289	28
	6/10	Fee		√	2.00		1287	28
424	6/17	Interest		√		51 49	1338	77
425	6/25	Car Payment	480 93				857	84
426	6/29	Phone	27 38				830	46

CHECKING ACCOUNT Monthly Statement		Account Number: 934-316-6	
Date	Transaction	Amount	Balance
6/1	OPENING BALANCE		1522.07
6/4	DEPOSIT	700.80	
6/4	CHECK	91.95	
6/4	CHECK	465.75	
6/7	CHECK	375.89	
6/10	FEE	2.00	
6/17	INTEREST	51.49	
6/24	CLOSING BALANCE		

(A) $1337.5   (B) $1338.77   (C) $1308.77   (D) $1138.77

85. Complete the check registry below. Find the balance showing after the last deposit and determine if the bank statement and the checkbook balance correctly. Explain your answer.

		RECORD ALL CHARGES OR CREDITS THAT AFFECT YOUR ACCOUNT							BALANCE	
NUMBER	DATE	DESCRIPTION OF TRANSACTION	PAYMENT/DEBIT (–)		√T	FEE (IF ANY) (–)	DEPOSIT/CREDIT (+)		1271	85
826	6/15	Mortgage	891	41	√					
	6/16	Deposit			√		1345	61		
827	6/18	Insurance	173	75	√					
828	6/19	Water	45	78	√					
829	6/23	Phone	35	71	√					
830	6/28	Eye Exam	115	50						
	6/30	Interest			√		54	21		
	6/30	Deposit					1345	61		

CHECKING ACCOUNT Monthly Statement			Account Number: 750-386-8	
Date	Transaction		Amount	Balance
6/14	OPENING BALANCE			1271.85
6/16	DEPOSIT		1345.61	2617.46
6/18	CHECK		891.41	1726.05
6/23	CHECK		46.78	1679.27
6/24	CHECK		173.75	1505.52
6/27	CHECK		35.71	1469.81
6/30	INTEREST		54.21	1524.02
6/30	CLOSING BALANCE			1524.02

Chapter 6 Applications for Business and Consumers

Section 6.1: Applications to Purchasing

Objective A: To find unit cost

[1] (C)

[2] (A)

[3] (B)

[4] (D)

[5] $237.00

Objective B: To find the most economical purchase

[6] (D)

[7] (D)

[8] (C)

[9] (D)

[10] $4 more per tube

Objective C: To find total cost

[11] (B)

[12] (B)

[13] (C)

[14] (B)

[15] $5.54 _____

Section 6.2: Percent Increase and Percent Decrease

Objective A: To find percent increase

[16] (C) _____

[17] (A) _____

[18] (A) _____

[19] (D) _____

[20] 14.8% _____

Objective B: To apply percent increase to business - markup

[21] (A) _____

[22] (B) _____

[23] (B) _____

[24] (C) _____

[25] 18% _____

Objective C: To find percent decrease

[26] (B) _____

[27] (C) _____

[28] (A) _____

[29] (A)

   a. 1998
[30] b. 71%

Objective D: To apply percent decrease to business - discount

[31] (D)

[32] (A)

[33] (C)

[34] (B)

[35] 20%

Section 6.3: Interest

Objective A: To calculate simple interest

[36] (D)

[37] (D)

[38] (B)

[39] (C)

[40] $1260

Objective B: To calculate finance charges on a credit card bill

[41] (A)

[42] (C)

[43] (C) _____

[44] (A) _____

[45] $6.78 _____

Objective C: To calculate compound interest

[46] (C) _____

[47] (A) _____

[48] (A) _____

[49] (D) _____

[50] $1673 _____

Section 6.4: Real Estate Expenses

Objective A: To calculate the initial expenses of buying a home

[51] (D) _____

[52] (C) _____

[53] (B) _____

[54] (C) _____

[55] $39,000 _____

Objective B: To calculate ongoing expenses of owning a home

[56] (C) _____

[57] (D)_____

[58] (A)_____

[59] (B)_____

[60] $152,000_____

Section 6.5: Car Expenses

Objective A: To calculate the initial expenses of buying a car

[61] (B)_____

[62] (D)_____

[63] (C)_____

[64] (C)_____

[65] $287.00_____

Objective B: To calculate ongoing expenses of owning a car

[66] (A)_____

[67] (C)_____

[68] (A)_____

[69] (B)_____

[70] $16,320; $286.14_____

Section 6.6: Wages

Objective A: To calculate commissions, total hourly wages, and salaries

[71] (A)

[72] (D)

[73] (C)

[74] (D)

[75] $286.45

Section 6.7: Bank Statements

Objective A: To calculate checkbook balances

[76] (A)

[77] (C)

[78] (D)

[79] (C)

[80] $1212.44

Objective B: To balance a checkbook

[81] (B)

[82] (C)

[83] (A)

[84] (B)

		RECORD ALL CHARGES OR CREDITS THAT AFFECT YOUR ACCOUNT							BALANCE	
NUMBER	DATE	DESCRIPTION OF TRANSACTION	PAYMENT/DEBIT (–)		√ T	FEE (IF ANY) (–)	DEPOSIT/CREDIT (+)			
826	6/15	Mortgage	891	41	√					
	6/16	Deposit			√		1345	61		
827	6/18	Insurance	173	75	√					
828	6/19	Water	45	78	√					
829	6/23	Phone	35	71	√					
830	6/28	Eye Exam	115	50						
	6/30	Interest			√					
	6/30	Deposit					1345	61		

The bank statement and the checkbook do not balance. The "Payment/Debit" was entered
[85] incorrectly for check number 828.

Chapter 7 Statistics and Probability

Section 7.1: Pictographs and Circle Graphs

Objective A: To read a pictorgraph

1. The pictograph shows the top 6 countries that won medals at the 1994 Commonwealth Games in Victoria, British Columbia.

Approximately how many more medals did Canada win than England?

(A) about 2   (B) about 3   (C) about 202   (D) about 4

2. The pictograph shows recent gold production throughout the world.

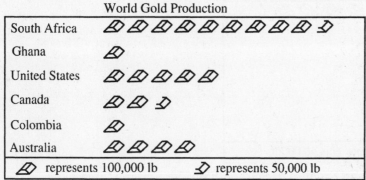

How many more pounds of gold were mined in Australia than in Canada?

(A) 160,000 lb   (B) 260,000 lb   (C) 150,000 lb   (D) 250,000 lb

3. The pictograph below shows the number of new homes built in a city. Use this pictograph to determine how many homes were built in the city in 1990.

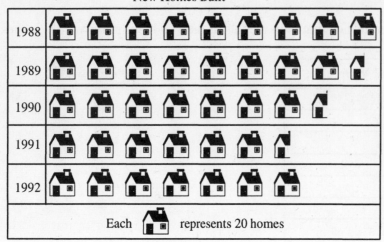

New Homes Built

(A) 150   (B) 7.5   (C) 160   (D) 130

4. The pictograph shows recent gold production throughout the world.

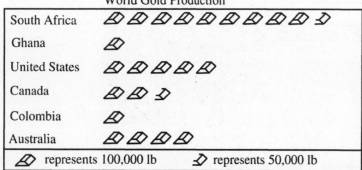

World Gold Production

Which is the ratio of gold production in South Africa to gold production in Colombia?

(A) $\dfrac{1}{19}$ (B) $\dfrac{19}{2}$ (C) $\dfrac{2}{19}$ (D) $\dfrac{9}{1}$

5. The picture below shows estimates of the population of four cities. Give the approximate population of Fairyland.

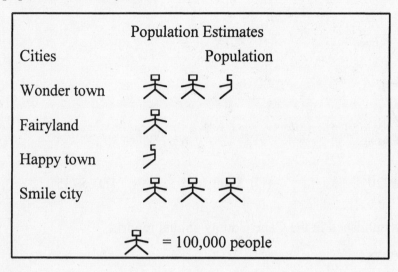

Population Estimates

Cities	Population
Wonder town	
Fairyland	
Happy town	
Smile city	

= 100,000 people

Objective B: To read a circle graph

6. In a young person's monthly budget, $150 is spent on food, $180 is spent on housing, and $270 is spent on other items. Which circle graph correctly represents this data?

(A)

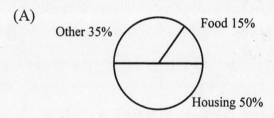

Other 35%   Food 15%

Housing 50%

(B)

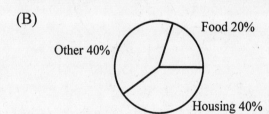

Food 20%

Other 40%

Housing 40%

(C)

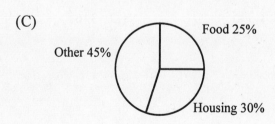

Other 45%   Food 25%

Housing 30%

(D) none of these

7. The circle graph below represents a family's monthly budget. If the total monthly income is $2100, how much money is spent on food?

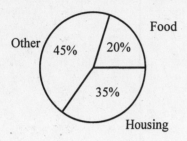

(A) $350   (B) $420   (C) $200   (D) $735

8. The following circle graph was published in the Cane County annual report.

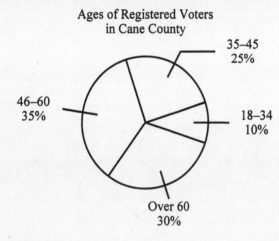

If there are 11,550 registered voters in Cane County, how many are over 60 years old?

(A) 2988   (B) 2888   (C) 3455   (D) 3465

9. There were 130,000 participants in a national taste test of four brands of cereal. Of the participants, 19,500 preferred brand A, 13,000 preferred brand B, 32,500 preferred brand C, and 65,000 preferred brand D. Which circle graph represents this data?

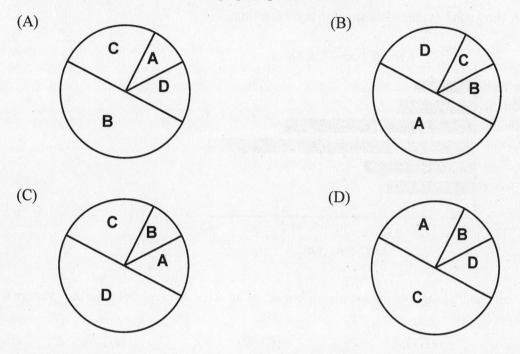

(A)

(B)

(C)

(D)

10. The ABC Company employs 200 people. The graph shows the distribution of the company's employees by job type.

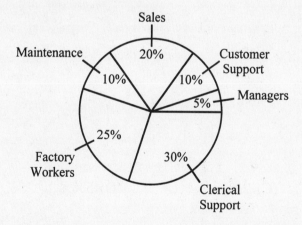

If raises in salary are given only to the customer support staff and factory workers, what fraction of the company's workforce will receive raises?

Section 7.2: Bar Graphs and Broken-Line Graphs

Objective A: To read a bar graph

11. The bar graph shows the average life span of several animals.

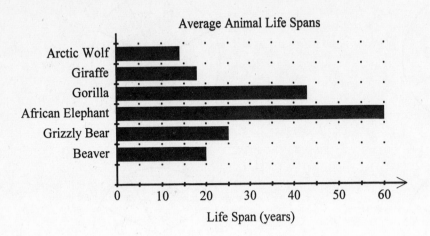

About how many years longer is the average life span of an African elephant than the average life span of a beaver?

(A) 35   (B) 6   (C) 40   (D) 46

12. The graph below shows the sales of various vehicles by one dealer for the month of March. Approximately what percent more sedans were sold than coupes?

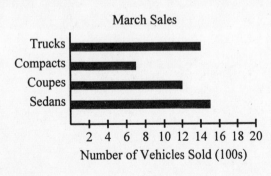

(A) 60%   (B) 20%   (C) 25%   (D) 5%

13. The table below shows the lowest and highest selling price of a stock during the first five days of January. Which of the following could be a selling price for that stock during the day of January 4th?

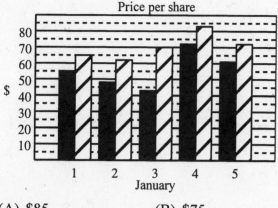

(A) $85   (B) $75   (C) $70   (D) $65

14. The manager of The Music Experience made the graph below to show the sales of tapes and CDs from 1997 to 2001.

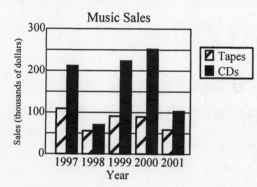

In what year was the difference in sales the greatest?

(A) 1998   (B) 1997   (C) 2000   (D) 1999

15. Use the following information to draw a bar graph showing the number of participants in the various school clubs.

Drama	Speech	Debate	Camera	Choir
40	85	50	20	60

Objective B: To read a broken-line graph

16. The graph below shows the tide levels during a six-hour period at the beach.

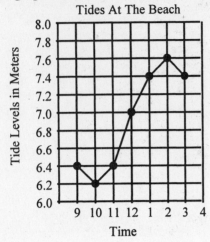

During what time period did the tide rise the greatest number of meters?

(A) Between 2 and 3

(B) Between 10 and 11

(C) Between 12 and 1

(D) Between 11 and 12

17. Which comparison line graph best matches the table of Acme Company profits for the first six months in 1997 and 1998?

Acme Co.	Jan.	Feb.	Mar.	Apr.	May	Jun.
1997 Profits	$3500	$2000	$3000	$4000	$3000	$4500
1998 Profits	$1500	$1000	$2500	$1500	$1000	$1000

(A)

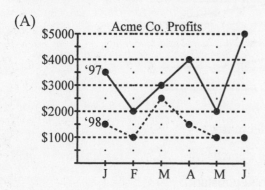

(B)

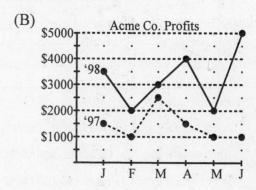

(C)

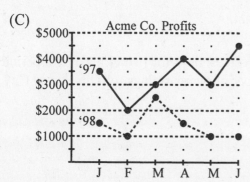

(D) none of these

18. Which statement describes the attendance rate from 1972 to 1978?

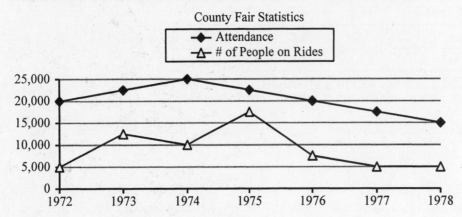

(A) There was a rapid increase and then a gradual decrease.

(B) There was a gradual increase and then a gradual decrease.

(C) There was a gradual increase and then it remained constant.

(D) The number of people attending remained constant.

19. The double-broken-line graph shows the number of overcast days for two cities over a period of five months. What is the difference between the number of overcast days for City A and City B for the month of February?

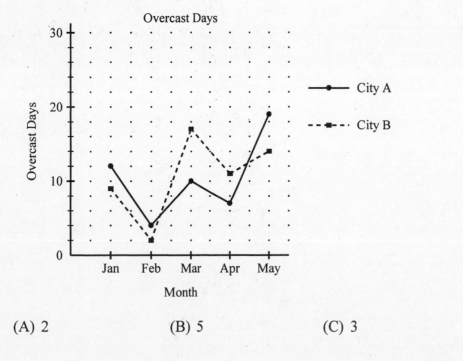

(A) 2   (B) 5   (C) 3   (D) 4

20. The double-broken-line graph shows the number of overcast days for two cities over a period of five months. What is the ratio of the number of overcast days for City B to the number of overcast days for City A for the month of February?

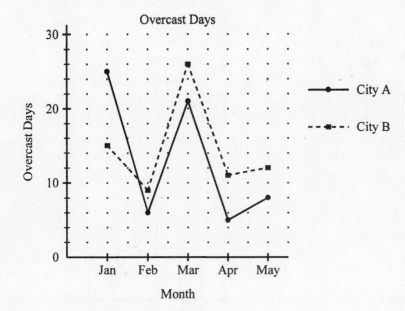

Section 7.3: Historgrams and Frequency Polygons

Objective A: To read a histogram

21. Use the histogram below to find the total frequency for the interval from 2.5 to 4.5.

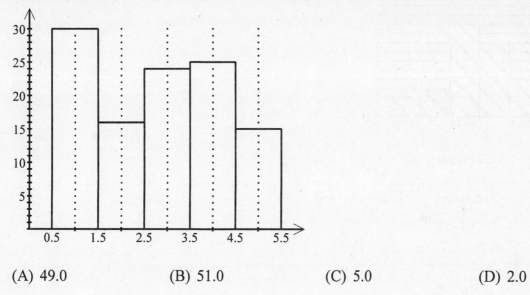

(A) 49.0　　　　(B) 51.0　　　　(C) 5.0　　　　(D) 2.0

22. The golf scores for the 27 members of the Belmont Country Club were 75, 86, 94, 119, 102, 98, 103, 71, 87, 111, 107, 99, 86, 78, 112, 95, 74, 83, 106, 85, 98, 94, 83, 99, 81, 97, 92. Make a histogram using ten-point intervals that shows the frequency distribution of the scores.

(A)

(B)

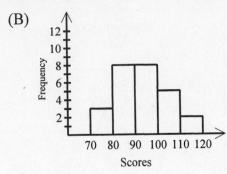

(C)

(D)

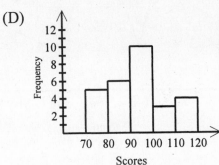

23. The histogram below shows the number of minutes students walked during a fund-raising walk. How many students walked for 10–19 minutes?

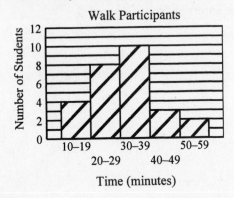

(A) 5   (B) 12   (C) 6   (D) 4

24. Which histogram accurately displays the data?

Number of Days of Rainfall		
Rainfall (cm)	Tally	Frequency
0.0-0.5	卌 卌 卌 卌 卌 IIII	29
0.6-1.1	卌 卌 卌 卌 II	22
1.2-1.7	卌 卌 III	13
1.8+	IIII	4

(A)
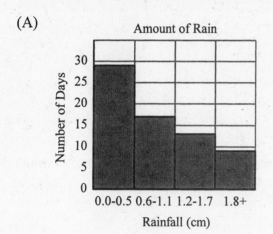

(B)
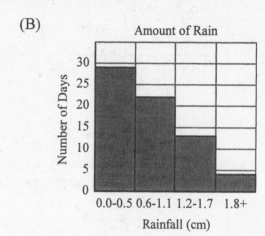

(C)
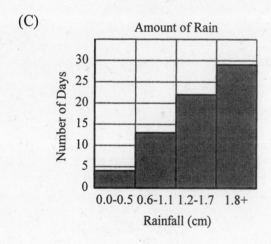

(D)
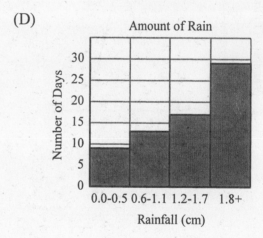

25. The test scores for the 28 members of the Advanced Math class are represented in the histogram below. How many students had scores between 110 and 119?

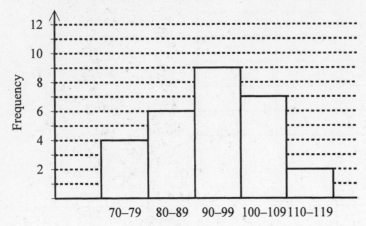

Objective B: To read a frequency polygon

26. The frequency polygon below shows the completion times for entrants in a 3200 meter running race. How many runners completed the race in under 9.5 minutes?

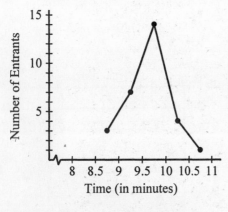

(A) 21   (B) 19   (C) 18   (D) 10

27. The golf scores for the 27 members of the Surrey Country Club were 94, 87, 108, 115, 73, 101, 72, 99, 116, 83, 94, 85, 78, 107, 86, 91, 79, 72, 97, 81, 96, 84, 85, 98, 99, 92, 93. Which frequency polygon correctly shows the frequency distribution of the scores using ten-point intervals?

(A)

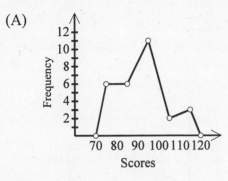

(B)

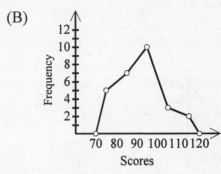

(C)

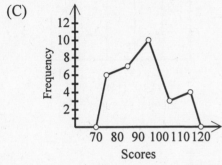

(D)

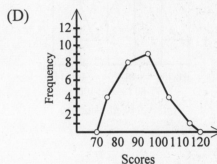

28. The frequency polygon below shows the one-way distance traveled to and from work by a sample of 74 city residents. What percent of the residents commute between 0 and 30 miles each way to and from work?

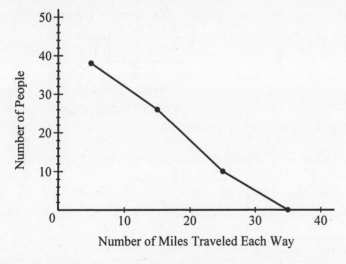

(A) 100.0%   (B) 0.0%   (C) 50.7%   (D) 56.2%

29. On a certain day in July, the high temperatures in 13 European cities were compiled into this table.

Temperature interval F°	61 – 70	71 – 80	81 – 90	90 – 100	100 – 110
Frequency	1	4	3	1	4

Which graph shows the frequency histogram and frequency polygon for the given data?

(A)

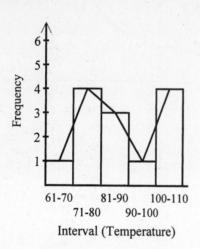

(B)

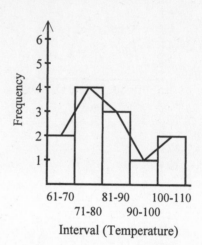

(C)

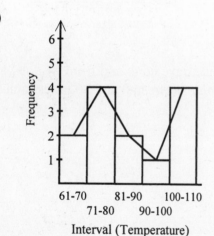

(D)

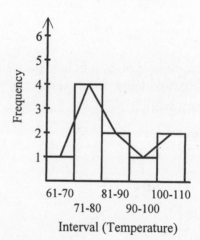

30. On a certain day in July, the high temperatures in 17 European cities were compiled into this table.

Temperature interval °F	61 – 70	71 – 80	81 – 90	90 – 100	100 – 110
Frequency	2	2	6	1	6

a. Construct a frequency histogram from the given data.

b. Draw the frequency line on this histogram.

Section 7.4: Statistical Measures

Objective A: To find the mean, median, and mode of a distribution

31. You weigh six packages and find the weights to be 18, 12, 42, 15, 39, and 36 ounces. If you include a package that weighs 132 ounces, which will increase more, the median or the mean?

(A) The mean increases more.

(B) The median and mean are affected the same amount.

(C) The median increases more.

(D) The median and the mean will stay the same.

32. What are the mean, median, and mode of the data in the following sample?
7, 7, 15, 3, 9, 15, 15, 17

(A) 12, 11, 15   (B) 12, 15, 11   (C) 11, 12, 15   (D) 11, 21, 15

33. The number of patients treated in a dental office each day was recorded for 11 days. Find the mean, the median, and the mode for this data.
6, 27, 15, 20, 17, 23, 23, 10, 22, 23, 12

(A) 18, 23, 20   (B) 20, 18, 23   (C) 20.5, 18, 23   (D) 18, 20, 23

34. In a mathematics class, half of the students scored 91 on an achievement test. With the exception of a few students who scored 53, the remaining students scored 73. Which of the following statements is true about the distribution of scores?

(A) The mean and the median are the same.

(B) The mean is less than the median.

(C) The mean is greater than the median.

(D) The mean is greater than the mode.

35. For the first three sets of numbers below, the value of x represents the same type of measure of central tendency. Find the value of x for the fourth set of numbers.

5	4	24	13
20	8	26	17
25	32	26	17
30	36	26	21
50	44	30	21
	52		23

$x = 25$ $x = 34$ $x = 26$ $x = \underline{}$

Objective B: To draw a box-and-whiskers plot

36. Draw a box-and-whisker plot for the following data.
38, 34, 26, 17, 28, 29, 25, 23, 32, 19, 20, 38, 18, 28, 18

(A)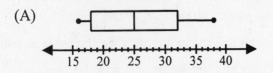

(B)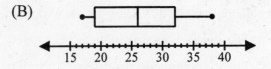

(C)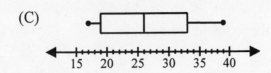

(D)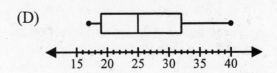

37. Mrs. Myers drew a box-and-whisker plot to represent her students' scores on a midterm test.

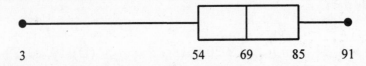

Julie earned 54 on the test. Describe how the scores of Julie's classmates compared to Julie's score.

(A) about $\frac{1}{4}$ scored higher; about $\frac{3}{4}$ scored lower

(B) about $\frac{1}{2}$ scored higher; about $\frac{1}{2}$ scored lower

(C) about $\frac{3}{4}$ scored higher; about $\frac{1}{2}$ scored lower

(D) about $\frac{3}{4}$ scored higher; about $\frac{1}{4}$ scored lower

38. Which statement is *not* true about the data shown by the box-and-whisker plot below?

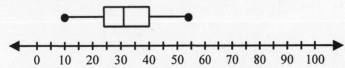

(A) Half the data lies between 31 and 40.   (B) One fourth of the data is less than 24.

(C) The data point 45 lies in the fourth quartile of the data.   (D) The range is 44.

39. The box-and-whisker plots show data for test scores in a classroom. Which plot represents data in which 25% of the class earned below 60%?

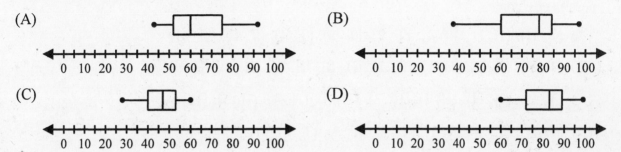

(A)

(B)

(C)

(D)

40. Find the range and interquartile range for the data represented by the box-and-whisker plot.

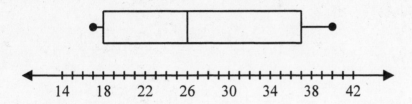

Section 7.5: Introduction to Probability

Objective A: To calculate the probability of simple events

41. You work at a T-shirt printing business. Of 1300 T-shirts shipped, 91 are printed improperly. If you choose a T-shirt out of the shipment, what is the chance that it is printed correctly?

(A) 0.91%   (B) 13%   (C) 7%   (D) 93%

42. A bag contains 2 red marbles, 5 white marbles, and 7 blue marbles. Find the probability of obtaining a white or a blue marble in a single draw.

(A) $\dfrac{9}{14}$ (B) $\dfrac{1}{2}$ (C) $\dfrac{6}{7}$ (D) 1

43. A coin is tossed. If a head appears, a spinner that can land on any of the numbers from 1 to 6 is spun. If a tail appears, the coin is tossed a second time instead of spinning the spinner. What are the possible outcomes?

(A) (T, H), (H, H), (T, 1), (T, 2), (T, 3), (T, 4), (T, 5), (T, 6)

(B) (T, H), (T, T), (H, 1), (H, 2), (H, 3), (H, 4), (H, 5), (H, 6)

(C) (T, H), (H, H), (H, 1), (H, 2), (H, 3), (H, 4), (H, 5), (H, 6)

(D) (T, H), (T, T), (T, 1), (T, 2), (T, 3), (T, 4), (T, 5), (T, 6)

44. Two urns each contain black balls and blue balls. Urn I contains five black balls and six blue balls. Urn II contains four black balls and three blue balls. A ball is drawn from each urn. What is the probability that both balls are black?

(A) $\dfrac{3}{13}$ (B) $\dfrac{9}{79}$ (C) $\dfrac{9}{80}$ (D) $\dfrac{20}{77}$

45. From a committee of 7 girls and 6 boys, two names are drawn to lead the committee. What is the probability that both people drawn will be boys?

Chapter 7 Statistics and Probability

Section 7.1: Pictographs and Circle Graphs

Objective A: To read a pictorgraph

[1] (A)

[2] (C)

[3] (A)

[4] (B)

[5] 100,000

Objective B: To read a circle graph

[6] (C)

[7] (B)

[8] (D)

[9] (C)

[10] $\dfrac{7}{20}$

Section 7.2: Bar Graphs and Broken-Line Graphs

Objective A: To read a bar graph

[11] (C)

[12] (C)

[13] (B)

[14] (C)

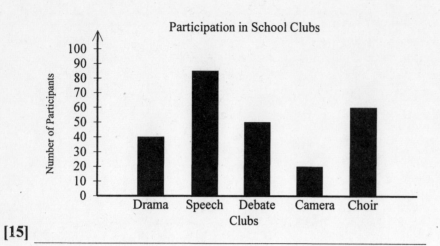

[15] _____

Objective B: To read a broken-line graph

[16] (D)

[17] (C)

[18] (B)

[19] (A)

[20] $\dfrac{3}{2}$ _____

Section 7.3: Historgrams and Frequency Polygons

Objective A: To read a histogram

[21] (A)

[22] (A)

[23] (D)

[24] (B)

[25] 2

Objective B: To read a frequency polygon

[26] (D)

[27] (B)

[28] (A)

[29] (A)

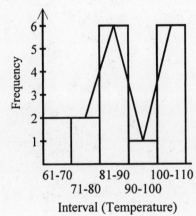

[30]

Section 7.4: Statistical Measures

Objective A: To find the mean, median, and mode of a distribution

[31] (A)

[32] (C)

[33] (D)

[34] (B)

[35] 19

Objective B: To draw a box-and-whiskers plot

[36] (B)

[37] (D)

[38] (A)

[39] (B)

[40] range = 23
interquartile range = 19

Section 7.5: Introduction to Probability

Objective A: To calculate the probability of simple events

[41] (D)

[42] (C)

[43] (B)

[44] (D)

[45] $\dfrac{5}{26}$

Chapter 8 U.S. Customary Units of Measurement

Section 8.1: Length

Objective A: To convert measurements of length in the U.S. Customary System

Convert.

1. 2 ft = ___ in.

    (A) 20   (B) 24   (C) 6   (D) 8

2. 6 yd = ___ in.

    (A) 18   (B) 75   (C) 72   (D) 216

3. $23\frac{1}{2}$ ft = ___ yd

    (A) $8\frac{1}{6}$ (B) $7\frac{5}{6}$ (C) $70\frac{1}{2}$ (D) 282

4. $2\frac{2}{3}$ yd = ___ ft

    (A) $6\frac{2}{3}$ (B) 8   (C) 96   (D) 32

5. 42,240 ft = ___ mi

Objective B: To perform arithmetic operations with measurement of length

6. Convert 13 yd 1 ft to feet.

    (A) 16 ft   (B) 157 ft   (C) 27 ft   (D) 40 ft

7. Divide 42 ft 11 in. by 5.

    (A) 9 ft 7 in.   (B) 8 ft 7 in.   (C) 8 ft 8 in.   (D) 9 ft 8 in.

8. Multiply 4 ft 8 in. by 4.

    (A) 17 ft 7 in.   (B) 18 ft 8 in.   (C) 18 ft 7 in.   (D) 17 ft 8 in.

9. Complete.

   40 in. = ___ ft ___ in.

   (A) 3, 7   (B) 4, 4   (C) 3, 4   (D) 4, 7

10. Multiply 3 ft 5 in. by 5.

Objective C: To solve application problems

11. A carpenter cuts 5 feet 5 inches from a board of length 10 feet 3 inches. Which is the length of the board after the cut?

   (A) 6 ft 2 in.   (B) 5 ft 10 in.   (C) 4 ft 2 in.   (D) 4 ft 10 in.

12. Julianne wants to cut a piece of plywood that is $6\frac{3}{4}$ feet long into 9-inch-wide strips. How many inches are equivalent to $6\frac{3}{4}$ feet?

   (A) 27 in.   (B) 66 in.   (C) 81 in.   (D) 57 in.

13. As shown in this diagram, the picture is not centered on the wall. How far left should it be moved to be centered?

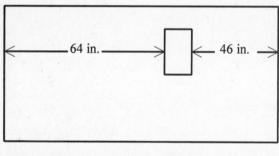

   (A) 11 in.   (B) 6 in.   (C) 18 in.   (D) 9 in.

14. The Stuarts bought a new couch that measures 6 feet long. The Stuarts' end tables are each 22 inches wide. How much space (length) is needed for one couch and two end tables?

   (A) 7 ft 7 in.   (B) 8 ft 7 in.   (C) 8 ft 8 in.   (D) 9 ft 8 in.

15. A carpenter cuts 4 feet 11 inches from a board of length 11 feet 7 inches. What is the length of the board after the cut?

Section 8.2: Weight

Objective A: To convert measurement of weight in the U.S. Customary System

Convert.

16. 160 oz = ___ lb

    (A) 100   (B) 10   (C) 2560   (D) 0.625

17. 48 oz = ___ lb

    (A) 480   (B) 192 lb   (C) 3   (D) 12

18. $70\frac{9}{10}$ tons = ___ lb

    (A) 141,800   (B) 70,450   (C) 140,900   (D) 70,900

19. 128 oz = ___ lb

    (A) 2   (B) 8   (C) 512   (D) 1280

20. $9\frac{5}{8}$ lb = ___ oz

Objective B: To perform arithmetic operations with measurements of weight

21. Divide 57 lb 4 oz by 4.

    (A) 15 lb 4 oz   (B) 14 lb $2\frac{1}{2}$ oz   (C) 14 lb 5 oz   (D) $28\frac{1}{2}$ lb 2 oz

22. Subtract 4 tons 1850 lb from 13 tons 860 lb.

    (A) 1846 tons 847 lb   (B) 9 tons 1010 lb   (C) 9 tons 990 lb   (D) 8 tons 1010 lb

Perform the arithmetic operation.

23. 185 lb 2 oz − 162 lb 13 oz

    (A) 23 lb 5 oz   (B) 22 lb 5 oz   (C) 23 lb 11 oz   (D) 22 lb 11 oz

Perform the arithmetic operation.

24. 8 lb 15 oz × 4

    (A) 35 lb 12 oz   (B) 35 lb 11 oz   (C) 34 lb 11 oz   (D) 36 lb 12 oz

25. 137 lb 5 oz − 110 lb 12 oz

Objective C: To solve application problems

26. One bag of Chock Full of Chips cookies weighs $9\frac{1}{4}$ ounces. How many pounds will a dozen bags weigh?

    (A) 9 lb 3 oz   (B) 11 lb 1 oz   (C) 6 lb 15 oz   (D) 7 lb

27. For a hobby club race, Roger made a kit car out of wood. He drilled a hole in the bottom of the car, which made the car 2 ounces lighter. Finally, Roger added tires that weighed a total of 4 ounces. At race time, the car weighed in at 9 ounces. How much did the car weigh at the beginning?

    (A) 4 oz   (B) 8 oz   (C) 9 oz   (D) 7 oz

28. An orca weighs about 4000 pounds. How many tons are in 4000 pounds?

    (A) 20 tons   (B) 4 tons   (C) 40 tons   (D) 2 tons

29. One box of cheddar rice cakes weighs $6\frac{1}{2}$ ounces. What will a dozen boxes weigh?

    (A) 4 lb 14 oz   (B) 7 lb 8 oz   (C) 8 lb 6 oz   (D) 4 lb

30. A hippo weighs about $3\frac{1}{2}$ tons. How many pounds are in $3\frac{1}{2}$ tons?

Section 8.3: Capacity

Objective A: To convert measurements of capacity in the U.S. Customary System

Convert.

31. 3 gal = ___ pt

    (A) 6   (B) 1.5   (C) 30   (D) 24

Convert.

32. 104 pt = ___ gal

    (A) 6.5   (B) 10.4   (C) 13   (D) 208

33. 18 qt = ___ gal

    (A) 26   (B) $3\frac{1}{2}$ (C) $4\frac{1}{2}$ (D) $5\frac{1}{2}$

34. 3 qt = ___ cups

    (A) 1.5   (B) 6   (C) 30   (D) 12

35. 3 qt = ___ cups

Objective B: To perform arithmetic operations with measurements of capacity

Perform the arithmetic operation.

36.
$$
\begin{array}{r}
7 \text{ qt } 7 \text{ pt} \\
\times \quad\quad 3 \\
\hline
\end{array}
$$

    (A) 42 qt   (B) 31 qt 1 pt   (C) 30 qt 1 pt   (D) 21 qt 7 pt

37.
$$
\begin{array}{r}
2 \text{ qt } 4 \text{ pt} \\
\times \quad\quad 3 \\
\hline
\end{array}
$$

    (A) 12 qt   (B) 18 qt   (C) 6 qt 4 pt   (D) 13 qt

38. $1\frac{2}{3}$ gal ÷ 6

    (A) $\frac{1}{6}$ gal   (B) $\frac{1}{3}$ gal   (C) $\frac{5}{18}$ gal   (D) 10 gal

39. 4 gal 2 qt − 2 gal 3 qt

    (A) 1 gal 3 qt   (B) 1 gal 2 qt   (C) 2 gal 2 qt   (D) 2 gal 3 qt

40. Perform the indicated operation.
9 gal 2 qt – 3 gal 3 qt

Objective C: To solve application problems

41. Mary's truck engine holds 3 gallons of oil. If there are 8 quarts of oil in the engine now, how many more quarts of oil does Mary need to add to fill the engine to capacity?

(A) 11   (B) 20   (C) 4   (D) 5

42. Kelly's secret soup recipe calls for $6\frac{1}{4}$ quarts of water. How many cups are equivalent to $6\frac{1}{4}$ quarts?

(A) 400   (B) 50   (C) 0.16   (D) 25

43. Jill needs $2\frac{1}{2}$ gallons of punch for a party. If she has 6 quarts of punch already, how many more quarts of punch does Jill need?

(A) 3   (B) 4   (C) 16   (D) 11

44. The recipe you are following calls for 8 quarts of water. You have 14 pints of water. Do you have enough water? If you have enough water, how much extra do you have? If you do not have enough, how much more do you need?

(A) No, 2 pt   (B) Yes, 2 pt   (C) No, 3 pt   (D) Yes, 3 pt

45. For a sports banquet, Jill must buy $2\frac{3}{4}$ gallons of soda. If she has 8 quarts of soda already, how many more quarts of soda does he need?

Section 8.4: Energy and Power

Objective A: To use units of energy in the U.S. Customary System

46. Convert 7030 foot-pounds to Btu. Use 1 Btu = 778 ft·lb.

(A) 5,469,360 Btu   (B) 9.136 Btu   (C) 5,469,340 Btu   (D) 9.036 Btu

47. Find the energy required to lift 2000 pounds a distance of 16 feet.

(A) 31,700 ft·lb　　(B) 32,000 ft·lb　　(C) 3200 ft·lb　　(D) 31,850 ft·lb

48. A furnace is rated at 20,000 Btu per hour. How many foot-pounds of energy does the furnace release in 2 hours? Use 1 Btu = 778 ft·lb.

(A) 31,120,000 ft·lb　　(B) 31,130,000 ft·lb　　(C) 31,100,000 ft·lb　　(D) 51.4 ft·lb

49. Five bales of cardboard must be moved 60 feet. If each bale weighs 70 pounds, find the amount of work required to move the cardboard.

(A) 4175 ft·lb　　(B) 21,000 ft·lb　　(C) 4200 ft·lb　　(D) 21,025 ft·lb

50. Convert 6650 foot-pounds to Btu. Use 1 Btu = 778 ft·lb.

Objective B: To use units of power in the U.S. Customary System

51. Convert $5225 \frac{\text{ft·lb}}{\text{s}}$ to horsepower. Use $1 \text{ hp} = 550 \frac{\text{ft·lb}}{\text{s}}$.

(A) 105 hp　　(B) 9.5 hp　　(C) 10.5 hp　　(D) 95 hp

52. Convert 1.5 horsepower to foot-pounds per second. Use $1 \text{ hp} = 550 \frac{\text{ft·lb}}{\text{s}}$.

(A) $1375 \frac{\text{ft·lb}}{\text{s}}$　　(B) $825 \frac{\text{ft·lb}}{\text{s}}$　　(C) $150 \frac{\text{ft·lb}}{\text{s}}$　　(D) $137.5 \frac{\text{ft·lb}}{\text{s}}$

53. Find the power in foot-pounds per second needed to raise 200 pounds a distance of 80 feet in 8 seconds.

(A) $2000 \frac{\text{ft·lb}}{\text{s}}$　　(B) $20 \frac{\text{ft·lb}}{\text{s}}$　　(C) $1970 \frac{\text{ft·lb}}{\text{s}}$　　(D) $128,000 \frac{\text{ft·lb}}{\text{s}}$

54. Find the power in foot-pounds per second of an engine that can raise 13,000 pounds to a height of 80 feet in 40 seconds.

(A) $6500 \frac{\text{ft·lb}}{\text{s}}$　　(B) $16,200 \frac{\text{ft·lb}}{\text{s}}$　　(C) $26,000 \frac{\text{ft·lb}}{\text{s}}$　　(D) $26,080 \frac{\text{ft·lb}}{\text{s}}$

55. A motor has a power of $8250 \frac{\text{ft·lb}}{\text{s}}$. Find the horsepower of the motor.

Chapter 8 U.S. Customary Units of Measurement

Section 8.1: Length

Objective A: To convert measurements of length in the U.S. Customary System

[1] (B)

[2] (D)

[3] (B)

[4] (B)

[5] 8

Objective B: To perform arithmetic operations with measurement of length

[6] (D)

[7] (B)

[8] (B)

[9] (C)

[10] 17 ft 1 in.

Objective C: To solve application problems

[11] (D)

[12] (C)

[13] (D)

[14] (D)

[15] 6 ft 8 in. _____

Section 8.2: Weight

Objective A: To convert measurement of weight in the U.S. Customary System

[16] (B) _____

[17] (C) _____

[18] (A) _____

[19] (B) _____

[20] 154 _____

Objective B: To perform arithmetic operations with measurements of weight

[21] (C) _____

[22] (D) _____

[23] (B) _____

[24] (A) _____

[25] 26 lb 9 oz _____

Objective C: To solve application problems

[26] (C) _____

[27] (D) _____

[28] (D) _____

[29] (A)

[30] 7000 lb

Section 8.3: Capacity

Objective A: To convert measurements of capacity in the U.S. Customary System

[31] (D)

[32] (C)

[33] (C)

[34] (D)

[35] 12

Objective B: To perform arithmetic operations with measurements of capacity

[36] (B)

[37] (A)

[38] (C)

[39] (A)

[40] 5 gal 3 qt

Objective C: To solve application problems

[41] (C)

[42] (D)

[43] (B)

[44] (A)

[45] 3 qt

Section 8.4: Energy and Power

Objective A: To use units of energy in the U.S. Customary System

[46] (D)

[47] (B)

[48] (A)

[49] (B)

[50] 8.548 Btu

Objective B: To use units of power in the U.S. Customary System

[51] (B)

[52] (B)

[53] (A)

[54] (C)

[55] 15 hp

Chapter 9 The Metric System of Measurement

Section 9.1: Length

Objective A: To convert units of length in the metric system of measurement

Convert.

1. 28.3 mm = ___ cm

   (A) 283   (B) 0.283   (C) 2830   (D) 2.83

2. 4 km = ___ m

   (A) 40,000   (B) 400   (C) 4000   (D) 40

3. 44.5 mm = ___ dm

   (A) 4.45   (B) 0.445   (C) 445   (D) 4450

4. 3.3 mm = ___ cm

   (A) 0.33   (B) 33   (C) 0.033   (D) 330

5. 72 cm = ___ m

Objective B: To solve application problems

6. The height of the ceiling in Mr. Johnson's classroom is 3.6 meters. How many centimeters is this?

   (A) 136   (B) 360   (C) 1036   (D) 36

7. A sunflower was 1.7 meters high one week ago. In 7 days it grew 29 centimeters. Find the current height of the sunflower.

   (A) 30.7 cm   (B) 30.82 cm   (C) 1.87 m   (D) 1.99 m

8. A chain is 24.6 centimeters long. What is its length in meters?

   (A) 2.46   (B) 2460   (C) 246   (D) 0.246

9. A statue stands 52.4 centimeters high. How many meters is this?

   (A) 5.24   (B) 0.0524   (C) 0.524   (D) 52.4

10. An outdoor plant was 0.7 meters high two weeks ago. In 14 days it grew 31 centimeters. Find the current height of the plant.

Section 9.2: Mass

Objective A: To convert units of mass in the metric system of measurement

Convert.

11. 6 mg = ___ g

    (A) 60   (B) 0.6   (C) 6000   (D) 0.006

12. 9 mg = ___ g

    (A) 9000   (B) 0.9   (C) 90   (D) 0.009

13. 2720 g = ___ kg

    (A) 27.2   (B) 2.72   (C) 0.272   (D) 0.0272

14. 1077 g = ___ mg

    (A) 107,700   (B) 1,077,000   (C) 10,770   (D) 10,770,000

15. 4.9 kg = ___ g

Objective B: To solve application problems

16. Kevin's science project worm had a mass of 1.8 grams one week ago. In 7 days it gained 19 centigrams. Find the mass of the worm now.

    (A) 20.8 cg   (B) 1.99 g   (C) 1.98 g   (D) 20.81 cg

17. A chemical weighs 2.4 kilograms. Which is its mass in milligrams?

    (A) 2,400,000   (B) 0.0000024   (C) 240,000   (D) 0.00000024

18. When Pablo takes his dog to the vet for a check-up, he finds out that his dog's mass is 27,000 grams. Which is the mass of the dog in kilograms?

    (A) 2.7   (B) 27   (C) 2700   (D) 270

19. A fish captured and released by a field biologist has a mass of 4.26 kilograms. Which is its mass in grams?

    (A) 4260   (B) 42,600   (C) 0.0426   (D) 42.6

20. A compost pile has a mass of 24 kilograms. Each day the compost pile loses 18 grams due to water evaporation. Find the total mass of the compost pile after four weeks.

Section 9.3: Capacity

Objective A: To converty units of capacity in the metric system of measurement

Convert.

21. 3.3 kl = ___ L

    (A) 0.33   (B) 3300   (C) 33   (D) 330

22. 374 ml = ___ L

    (A) 3.74   (B) 374,000   (C) 37,400   (D) 0.374

23. 150 L = ___ hl

    (A) 15   (B) 1.5   (C) 1500   (D) 0.15

24. 194 L = ___ ml

    (A) 194,000   (B) 19,400   (C) 0.194   (D) 1940

25. 76,000 dL = ___ L

Objective B: To solve application problems

26. A beaker contains 4.2 deciliters of acid. How many hectoliters of acid does it contain?

    (A) 0.00042   (B) 0.0042   (C) 4200   (D) 420

27. A barrel contains 10 liters of soda. How many milliliters of soda does it contain?

    (A) 100,000   (B) 1000   (C) 10,000   (D) 100

28. Ian has 1000 milliliters of water in some barrels. How many liters of water are in the barrels?

    (A) 100   (B) 10,000   (C) 1   (D) 10

29. A cup contains 25.7 milliliters of apple juice. How many liters of apple juice does it contain?

    (A) 0.257   (B) 25.7   (C) 0.0257   (D) 2.57

30. Sue poured 3000 milliliters of blue paint and 3000 milliliters of yellow paint into a bucket. How many liters of green paint were made?

Section 9.4: Energy

Objective A: To use units of energy in the metric system of measurement

31. How many Calories can you eliminate from your diet in 9 weeks by omitting 200 Calories per day?

    (A) 1790   (B) 12,500   (C) 12,600   (D) 1800

32. People whose daily activity level would be described as moderate need to consume 20 Calories per pound of body weight each day to maintain their weight. How many Calories should a 121-pound, moderately active person consume per day to maintain that weight?

    (A) 2420   (B) 2435   (C) 6   (D) 2445

33. For a healthy diet, it is recommended that 15% of the daily intake of Calories come from protein. Find the daily intake of Calories from protein that is appropriate if you want to limit your Calorie intake to 2300 Calories.

    (A) 34,500   (B) 345   (C) 360   (D) 1955

34. If playing softball requires 320 Calories per hour, how many Calories do you burn in 36 days playing 1 hour 45 minutes per day?

    (A) 11,520   (B) 12,096   (C) 80,640   (D) 20,160

35. After cross-country skiing for 5 hours, Sandra ate a meal containing 800 Calories. If cross-country skiing uses 520 Calories per hour, how many Calories did Sandra gain or lose from these two activities.

Section 9.5: Conversion Between the U.S. Customary and the Metric System of Measurement

Objective A: To convert U.S. Customary units to metric units

Convert.

36. Find the height in meters of a person 5 feet 5 inches tall.

    (A) 1.46   (B) 1.65   (C) 1.80   (D) 1.40

37. How many kilograms does a 4 pound chicken weigh?

    (A) 8.82   (B) 1.68   (C) 1.82   (D) 8.67

38. Find the number of liters in 8 cups of soda.

    (A) 3.32   (B) 33.76   (C) 1.89   (D) 2.00

39. A gallon of flat paint costs $20.33/gallon. Find the cost per liter.

    (A) $5.08   (B) $6.91   (C) $5.37   (D) $77.01

40. Sam drove home at an average speed of 27 mi/hr. Express this in kilometers per hour.

Objective B: To convert metric units to U.S. Customary units

Convert.

41. Convert a 1810 meter hike to feet.

    (A) 551.66 ft   (B) 5938.61 ft   (C) 6203.59 ft   (D) 603.33 ft

42. Find the number of gallons in 13 liters of water.

    (A) 3.25   (B) 49.24   (C) 52.00   (D) 3.43

43. Find the weight in pounds of a 401-kilogram cow.

    (A) 806.37   (B) 884.21   (C) 136.39   (D) 181.86

Convert.

44. Find the height in inches of a person 1.61 meters tall.

    (A) 63.39   (B) 55.42   (C) 57.96   (D) 56.69

45. How many gallons of water does a 23-liter tank hold? Round answer to nearest hundredths.

Chapter 9 The Metric System of Measurement

Section 9.1: Length

Objective A: To convert units of length in the metric system of measurement

[1] (D)

[2] (C)

[3] (B)

[4] (A)

[5] 0.72

Objective B: To solve application problems

[6] (B)

[7] (D)

[8] (D)

[9] (C)

[10] 1.01 m

Section 9.2: Mass

Objective A: To convert units of mass in the metric system of measurement

[11] (D)

[12] (D)

[13] (B)

[14] (B)

[15] 4900

Objective B: To solve application problems

[16] (B)

[17] (A)

[18] (B)

[19] (A)

[20] 23.496 kg

Section 9.3: Capacity

Objective A: To converty units of capacity in the metric system of measurement

[21] (B)

[22] (D)

[23] (B)

[24] (A)

[25] 7600

Objective B: To solve application problems

[26] (B)

[27] (C)

[28] (C)

[29] (C)

[30] 6

Section 9.4: Energy

Objective A: To use units of energy in the metric system of measurement

[31] (C)

[32] (A)

[33] (B)

[34] (D)

[35] loss of 1800 Calories

Section 9.5: Conversion Between the U.S. Customary and the Metric System of Measurement

Objective A: To convert U.S. Customary units to metric units

[36] (B)

[37] (C)

[38] (C)

[39] (C)

[40] 43.44 km/hr

Objective B: To convert metric units to U.S. Customary units

[41] (B)

[42] (D)

[43] (B)

[44] (A)

[45] 6.07

Chapter 10 Rational Numbers

Section 10.1: Introduction to Integers

Objective A: To identify the order relation between two integers

1. Which shows the numbers −18 and −13 graphed on a number line?

(A)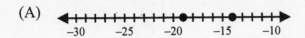

(B)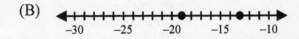

(C)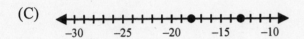

(D)

2. Which shows the numbers 6, 2 and −2 graphed on a number line?

(A)

(B)

(C)

(D)

3. Choose the correct symbol, >, <, or =. −22 ___ −45

   (A) >   (B) <   (C) =

4. Choose the correct symbol, >, <, or =. 98 ___ −131

   (A) >   (B) <   (C) =

5. Represent the quantity as an integer.
   An increase in temperature of ten degrees.

Objective B: To evaluate expressions that contain the absolute-value symbol

6. Find the opposite number of −4.

   (A) 4   (B) $\frac{1}{4}$ (C) −4   (D) $-\frac{1}{4}$

7. Find the opposite number of 18.

   (A) −18   (B) $\frac{1}{18}$ (C) $\frac{1}{-18}$ (D) 1

Evaluate.

8. $|20|$

   (A) $-\dfrac{1}{20}$
   (B) 20
   (C) $\dfrac{1}{20}$
   (D) -20

9. $-|-5|$

   (A) 5
   (B) ± 5
   (C) $\dfrac{1}{5}$
   (D) -5

10. $-|-12|$

Section 10.2: Addition and Subtraction of Integers

Objective A: To add integers

Add.

11. $-7+(-12)$

   (A) -5
   (B) -19
   (C) 19
   (D) 5

12. $8+(-16)$

   (A) 8
   (B) 24
   (C) -24
   (D) -8

13. $-20+14$

   (A) 6
   (B) -6
   (C) -34
   (D) 34

14. $(-26)+13+(-19)$

   (A) -20
   (B) 58
   (C) -32
   (D) 32

15. $(-6)+(-18)+19+(-23)$

Objective B: To subtract integers

Subtract.

16. $-14 - (-6)$

    (A) 8   (B) -8 (C) -20 (D) 20

17. $(-6) - (-7)$

    (A) 13   (B) 1   (C) -1 (D) -13

18. $-81 - 78 - (-91)$

    (A) -68 (B) -250 (C) 250   (D) 68

19. $-15 - 2 - (-6) - 21$

    (A) -28 (B) -44 (C) -32 (D) 10

20. $-20 - (-10) - (-57)$

Objective C: To solve application problems

21. Jasper is a pilot for Sky High Airlines. His three-week flight log showed that he traveled 6702 miles the first week, 6019 miles the second week, and 8694 miles the third week. How many miles did Jasper fly during this three-week period?

    (A) 21,415   (B) 20,414   (C) 22,525   (D) 21,305

22. The population of Texas in 1990 was 16,986,510. The population of Oregon in 1990 was 3,086,188. How many more people lived in Texas in 1990?

    (A) 13,900,322   (B) 13,660,322   (C) 13,900,342   (D) 13,901,322

23. The temperature in Duluth, Minnesota was $-18°$C at 6 A.M. By the afternoon, the temperature had risen $21°$C. By 6 P.M the temperature had fallen $13°$C. What was the temperature at 6 P.M.?

    (A) $13°$C   (B) $-10°$C   (C) $16°$C   (D) $-14°$C

24. Ryan has $157 in his savings account. He withdraws $110, deposits $45, and then withdraws $86. Which shows the ending balance of his account?

    (A) $-$6$ (B) $6   (C) $308   (D) $-$151$

25. Gail owns a small business. There was a profit of $13 on Wednesday and a loss of $18 on Thursday. On Friday there was a loss of $20, and on Saturday there was a profit of $17. Find the total profit or loss for the four days.

Section 10.3: Multiplication and Division of Integers

Objective A: To multiply integers

Multiply.

26. $10(-10)$

    (A) -20 (B) 20 (C) 100 (D) -100

27. $7(-5)$

    (A) 2 (B) 12 (C) -35 (D) 35

28. $(-5)8$

    (A) 3 (B) -40 (C) -13 (D) 40

29. $-1(12)(-5)$

    (A) 60 (B) 50 (C) -60 (D) -50

30. $(7)(-8)(-5)$

Objective B: To divide integers

Divide.

31. $(-28) \div 7$

    (A) -4 (B) $\dfrac{1}{4}$ (C) $-\dfrac{1}{4}$ (D) 4

32. $40 \div (-5)$

    (A) 8 (B) -8 (C) $\dfrac{1}{8}$ (D) $-\dfrac{1}{8}$

Divide.

33. $(-18) \div 3$

(A) $\dfrac{1}{6}$ (B) $-\dfrac{1}{6}$ (C) -6 (D) 6

34. $24 \div (-4)$

(A) 6 (B) -6 (C) $-\dfrac{1}{6}$ (D) $\dfrac{1}{6}$

35. $220 \div (-55)$

Objective C: To solve application problems

36. One day at 3:00 A.M., the temperature was –19°F in Juneau, Alaska. At 11:00 A.M. the temperature was –3°F. Which shows the average change in temperature per hour?

(A) $3°F$ (B) $16°F$ (C) $2°F$ (D) $-22°F$

37. A deep-sea diver must descend and ascend in short steps to equalize pressure on her body. Suppose the diver descends to the bottom in four steps of 12 feet each. How far did the diver descend?

(A) 48 ft   (B) 16 ft   (C) 8 ft   (D) 3 ft

38. Mindy ordered 40 boxes of nails from a hardware company. Each box contains 227 nails. How many nails did Mindy order?

(A) 7980   (B) 8060   (C) 10,130   (D) 9080

39. An art exhibit lasted 16 days. During that time, 5984 people visited the exhibit. On average, how many people visited each day?

(A) 6000   (B) 5968   (C) 352   (D) 374

40. At noon the temperature was 17°C. If the temperature then dropped 3°C per hour, what was the temperature at 5 P.M.?

Section 10.4: Operations with Rational Numbers

Objective A: To add or subtract rational numbers

Simplify.

41. $\dfrac{5}{6} + \dfrac{7}{9}$

(A) $-\dfrac{1}{18}$ (B) $1\dfrac{11}{18}$ (C) $\dfrac{1}{18}$ (D) $-1\dfrac{11}{18}$

42. $-\dfrac{14}{3} + \dfrac{13}{5} - \left(-\dfrac{12}{6}\right)$

(A) $9\dfrac{4}{15}$ (B) $7\dfrac{4}{15}$ (C) $1\dfrac{1}{13}$ (D) $-\dfrac{1}{15}$

43. $17.66 - 16.41 + 6.2$

(A) 22.61   (B) 1.25   (C) 23.86   (D) 7.45

44. $444.18 - 15.6$

(A) 428.58   (B) 288.18   (C) 44,262   (D) 459.78

45. $\dfrac{1}{5} + \dfrac{9}{25}$

Objective B: To multiply or divide rational numbers

Simplify.

46. $\dfrac{4}{7} \div \left(-\dfrac{7}{21}\right)$

(A) $-1\dfrac{5}{7}$ (B) $-\dfrac{4}{21}$ (C) $1\dfrac{5}{7}$ (D) $\dfrac{4}{21}$

Simplify.

47. $\dfrac{6}{7} \div \left(-\dfrac{2}{7}\right)$

    (A) 3   (B) -3 (C) $\dfrac{12}{49}$ (D) $-\dfrac{12}{49}$

48. $-\dfrac{20}{13} \times \dfrac{8}{5}$

    (A) $-2\dfrac{6}{13}$ (B) $-\dfrac{12}{65}$ (C) $-5\dfrac{1}{5}$ (D) $3\dfrac{1}{13}$

49. -7×0.019

    (A) -0.0133 (B) -0.133 (C) -13.3 (D) -1.33

50. $15.5 \div (-3.1)$

Objective C: To solve application problems

51. The temperature on February 3 in Bend, Oregon, was 35.2°F. On June 3, the temperature in Bend was 59.0°F. Find the differences in temperature on these two days.

    (A) 22.8°F   (B) 23.8°F   (C) 94.2°F   (D) 33.8°F

52. The weight of a chemical sample and its container is 67.83 grams. If the container has a weight of 28.706 grams, which is the weight of the sample?

    (A) 39.124 g   (B) 39.114 g   (C) 39.134 g   (D) 39.024 g

53. Gadget Manufacturing had stock that sold at $38\dfrac{7}{8}$ points. The stock fell $3\dfrac{1}{4}$ points. Which is the new stock value?

    (A) $42\dfrac{1}{8}$ points   (B) $35\dfrac{11}{16}$ points   (C) $35\dfrac{5}{8}$ points   (D) $42\dfrac{1}{16}$ points

54. This table shows the recent price trends for a group of stocks.

52-Week High Low		Stock-Div	High	Low	Last	Change
$23\frac{5}{8}$	$13\frac{1}{2}$	Chryslr 1.20	$15\frac{5}{8}$	15	$15\frac{1}{2}$	$-\frac{1}{4}$
$52\frac{1}{2}$	$35\frac{1}{4}$	Chubbs 1.32	45	43	$44\frac{1}{2}$	$-\frac{3}{4}$
$5\frac{5}{8}$	$1\frac{1}{2}$	Chyron	3	$2\frac{1}{8}$	3	...
$40\frac{1}{8}$	$32\frac{5}{8}$	Cilcorp 2.46	$32\frac{7}{8}$	$32\frac{1}{4}$	$32\frac{1}{4}$	$-\frac{5}{8}$
36	23	Cinnbel .76	$25\frac{3}{8}$	25	$25\frac{1}{8}$	...
$33\frac{3}{8}$	$28\frac{1}{4}$	CinGE 2.40	$29\frac{1}{2}$	29	29	$-\frac{5}{8}$
47	39	CinG pf 4.00	46	46	46	$+1$
$22\frac{3}{4}$	16	CinMil .72	$18\frac{7}{8}$	$18\frac{5}{8}$	$18\frac{7}{8}$	$+\frac{1}{8}$
$12\frac{1}{2}$	$3\frac{3}{8}$	CineOd	$6\frac{1}{4}$	6	$6\frac{1}{4}$	...

Using the table, determine the closing price of CinMil stock on the day before the table was published.

(A) $18\frac{5}{8}$ (B) $18\frac{3}{4}$ (C) 19 (D) 18

55. There are 35.12 grams of medication. If a pharmacist wants to separate the medication into 36 capsules, how many grams will be in each? Round to the nearest hundredth.

Section 10.5: Scientific Notation and the Order of Operations Agreement

Objective A: To write a number in scientific notation

Express the number in scientific notation.

56. 45,000,000

(A) 4.5×10^8 (B) 45×10^6 (C) 4.5×10^7 (D) 4.5×10^9

Express the number in scientific notation.

57. 0.00000883

    (A) 8.83×10^{-4} (B) 8.83×10^{7} (C) 883×10^{-6} (D) 8.83×10^{-6}

Express the number in decimal notation.

58. 7.68×10^{3}

    (A) 76,800   (B) 768   (C) 0.00768   (D) 7680

59. 8.68×10^{7}

    (A) 0.000000868   (B) 86,800,000   (C) 8,680,000   (D) 868,000,000

60. A virus takes up a volume of approximately 0.000000000000015 cubic centimeter. Write the number in scientific notation.

Objective B: To use the Order of Operations Agreement to simplify expressions

Simplify.

61. $9 + 2^{2} - (5 + 6)$

    (A) 2   (B) 110   (C) 122   (D) 14

62. $9.6 \times 17.2 + 0.8 \div 4$

    (A) 82.96   (B) 43.2   (C) 169.12   (D) 165.32

63. $\left(\dfrac{1}{6} + \dfrac{6}{5}\right)\left(\dfrac{11}{30} - \dfrac{1}{6}\right)$

    (A) $1\dfrac{17}{30}$ (B) $\dfrac{41}{150}$ (C) $\dfrac{11}{25}$ (D) $\dfrac{164}{225}$

64. $\left(\dfrac{9}{4}\right)^{2} - \dfrac{15}{4} \cdot \dfrac{8}{5}$

    (A) $1\dfrac{49}{80}$ (B) $2\dfrac{1}{10}$ (C) $-\dfrac{15}{16}$ (D) $-\dfrac{73}{80}$

Simplify.

65. $3 \cdot 4 + 12 - 6 \div 2 + 2(7 - 3)$

Chapter 10 Rational Numbers

Section 10.1: Introduction to Integers

Objective A: To identify the order relation between two integers

[1] (C)

[2] (B)

[3] (A)

[4] (A)

[5] 10

Objective B: To evaluate expressions that contain the absolute-value symbol

[6] (A)

[7] (A)

[8] (B)

[9] (D)

[10] -12

Section 10.2: Addition and Subtraction of Integers

Objective A: To add integers

[11] (B)

[12] (D)

[13] (B)

[14] (C)

[15] −28

Objective B: To subtract integers

[16] (B)

[17] (B)

[18] (A)

[19] (C)

[20] 47

Objective C: To solve application problems

[21] (A)

[22] (A)

[23] (B)

[24] (B)

[25] $8 loss

Section 10.3: Multiplication and Division of Integers

Objective A: To multiply integers

[26] (D)

[27] (C)

[28] (B)

[29] (A)

[30] 280

Objective B: To divide integers

[31] (A)

[32] (B)

[33] (C)

[34] (B)

[35] -4

Objective C: To solve application problems

[36] (C)

[37] (A)

[38] (D)

[39] (D)

[40] $2°C$

Section 10.4: Operations with Rational Numbers

Objective A: To add or subtract rational numbers

[41] (B)

[42] (D)

[43] (D)

[44] (A)

[45] $\dfrac{14}{25}$

Objective B: To multiply or divide rational numbers

[46] (A)

[47] (B)

[48] (A)

[49] (B)

[50] -5

Objective C: To solve application problems

[51] (B)

[52] (A)

[53] (C)

[54] (B)

[55] 0.98

Section 10.5: Scientific Notation and the Order of Operations Agreement

Objective A: To write a number in scientific notation

[56] (C)

[57] (D)

[58] (D)

[59] (B)

[60] 1.5×10^{-14} cm^3

Objective B: To use the Order of Operations Agreement to simplify expressions

[61] (A)

[62] (D)

[63] (B)

[64] (C)

[65] 29

Chapter 11 Introduction to Algebra

Section 11.1: Variable Expressions

Objective A: To evaluate variable expressions

1. Evaluate $a - b + c$ when $a = -3$, $b = -5$, and $c = 1$.

   (A) 1   (B) -9 (C) -7 (D) 3

2. Evaluate $x - y$ when $x = -\dfrac{4}{3}$ and $y = \dfrac{5}{2}$.

   (A) $\dfrac{7}{6}$ (B) $-\dfrac{23}{6}$ (C) $-\dfrac{7}{6}$ (D) $\dfrac{23}{6}$

3. Evaluate $2cd + c^2$ when $c = -5$ and $d = -8$.

   (A) -5625 (B) 105   (C) -105 (D) 5625

4. Evaluate $\dfrac{2}{3}a - 3b + 4a$ when $a = 3$ and $b = 6$.

   (A) -21 (B) -4 (C) 0   (D) 39

5. Evaluate $rs - (r - s)$ when $r = 0.5$ and $s = 0.4$.

Objective B: To simplify variable expressions containing no parenthesis

Simplify.

6. $4x + 8x$

   (A) $12x^2$ (B) $4x$ (C) $x + 12$ (D) $12x$

7. $7a - 4a + 7a$

   (A) $-4a$ (B) $10a$ (C) $-18a$ (D) $18a$

8. $-17b + 5a - 2b + 2a$

   (A) $10a + 34b$ (B) $-15a + 3b$ (C) $7a - 19b$ (D) $-12a$

9. $-7x^2 - 8x + 2x^2 - 5x^4$

   (A) $-5x^4 - 5x^2 - 8x$ (B) $2x^4 - 5x^2 - 8x$ (C) $-7x^4 - 5x^2 + 2x$ (D) in simplest form

Simplify.

10. $-2x^2 - 2x^4 - 3x^4$

Objective C: To simplify variable expressions containing parentheses

Simplify.

11. $-8(x-5)+4x$

(A) $12x+40$ (B) $-4x+40$ (C) $-4x-40$ (D) $-4x-5$

12. $8(x-8)+7(x-11)$

(A) $15x+13$ (B) $x+13$ (C) $x-141$ (D) $15x-141$

13. $7x-8(x+1)$

(A) $-x+8$ (B) $-x+1$ (C) $15x-8$ (D) $-x-8$

14. $-1-5(-5+x)+3x$

(A) $-2x+26$ (B) $-2x+24$ (C) $30-3x$ (D) $-6+30x$

15. $3x-2(x+4)$

Section 11.2: Introduction to Equations

Objective A: To determine whether a given value is a solution of an equation

16. Which number is a solution to the equation $4x-1=-2$?

(A) -1 (B) $-\dfrac{3}{4}$ (C) -3 (D) $-\dfrac{1}{4}$

17. Which number is a solution to the equation $-2x-9=-6x-29$?

(A) -6 (B) 5 (C) 6 (D) -5

18. Which number is a solution to the equation $8x+2=11x-10$?

(A) 3 (B) -3 (C) 4 (D) -4

19. Which number is a solution to the equation $2.06 = 2.63 - x$?

    (A) 0.57   (B) 1.57   (C) 3.06   (D) 4.69

20. Is 4 the solution to $3x - 5 = 7$?

Objective B: To solve an equation of the form x + a = b

Solve.

21. $s - 4 = 8$

    (A) −12   (B) −7   (C) 4   (D) 12

22. $29 = m - 2$

    (A) 27   (B) 31   (C) 58   (D) 30

23. $x + 3 = -1$

    (A) 4   (B) −4   (C) −2   (D) 2

24. $x - \dfrac{2}{9} = \dfrac{6}{12}$

    (A) $6\dfrac{1}{2}$ (B) $\dfrac{13}{18}$ (C) $\dfrac{2}{27}$ (D) $8\dfrac{2}{3}$

25. $18 = m + 6$

Objective C: To solve an equation of the form ax = b

Solve.

26. $9x = 63$

    (A) $\dfrac{1}{567}$ (B) 567   (C) 7   (D) $\dfrac{1}{7}$

27. $55 = -8y$

    (A) 63   (B) $\dfrac{55}{8}$ (C) −63   (D) $-\dfrac{55}{8}$

Solve.

28. $-\dfrac{7}{3}x = -1$

    (A) -4 (B) 21 (C) $\dfrac{3}{7}$ (D) $-\dfrac{4}{7}$

29. $-4x + 9x = 10$

    (A) 2 (B) 3 (C) -2 (D) -3

30. $-23 = -3y$

Objective D: To solve application problems

31. The density of a block of wood is 0.71 grams per cubic centimeter. What is the volume of the block if its mass is 23 grams?

    (A) 16.3 cm^3 (B) 0.031 cm^3 (C) 94 cm^3 (D) 32.4 cm^3

32. Pier 14 is 306 feet long. By how many feet must the pier be lengthened if the port authorities want to make it 368 feet long?

    (A) 62 (B) 52 (C) 112 (D) 162

33. The Phillipses traveled 415.2 miles on a trip to their grandma's house. At the end of the trip, the odometer read 15,996 miles. How many miles were on the odometer at the beginning of the trip?

    (A) $15,590.8$ (B) $15,580.8$ (C) $16,411.2$ (D) $16,311.2$

34. If 1260 students will be evenly distributed between 36 classes, how many students will be in each class?

    (A) 36 (B) 41 (C) 39 (D) 35

35. There were 759 runners preregistered for a race. More runners signed up the day of the race. If 1171 people ran in the race, how many runners signed up the day of the race?

Section 11.3: General Equations: Part 1

Objective A: To solve an equation of the form ax + b = c

Solve.

36. $5x + 20 = 10$

   (A) -2 (B) -3 (C) -7 (D) 6

37. $-3x - 6 = -24$

   (A) 6 (B) 4 (C) -9 (D) -15

38. $-2.5x - 1.8 = 2.3$

   (A) -1.64 (B) -0.2 (C) -2.04 (D) 6.6

39. $\frac{1}{5}y - 4 = 6$

   (A) -50 (B) -2 (C) 50 (D) 2

40. $-5x - 5 = 5$

Objective B: To solve application problems

41. Lawn ornaments may be rented at a rate determined by the formula $C = 2.7n + 1.9$, where C is the cost in dollars and n is the number of ornaments. Find the cost of renting 20 flamingo ornaments for a birthday party.

   (A) \$59.13   (B) \$52.10   (C) \$54.00   (D) \$55.90

42. The cost of renting a car is given by the formula $C = 50n + 0.15d$, where C is the cost in dollars, n is the number of days the car is rented, and d is the distance driven in kilometers. How much should you budget to rent a car for a 6-day trip, if you plan to drive 500 kilometers each day?

   (A) \$365.00   (B) \$375.00   (C) \$850.00   (D) \$750.00

43. Elena has \$7.70 in nickels and quarters. She has twice as many quarters as nickels. How many nickels and how many quarters does she have?

   (A) 12 nickels and 71 quarters   (B) 14 nickels and 28 quarters

   (C) 12 nickels and 24 quarters   (D) 28 nickels and 14 quarters

44. The relationship between Fahrenheit temperature and Celsius temperature is given by the formula $F = \dfrac{9}{5}C + 32$, where F is the Fahrenheit temperature and C is the Celsius temperature. Find C when $F = -31°$.

(A) $-315°$ (B) $-35°$ (C) $-49°$ (D) $1°$

45. Diane has \$2.24 in pennies and nickels. She has three times as many nickels as pennies. How many pennies and how many nickels does she have?

Section 11.4: General Equations: Part 2

Objective A: To solve an equation of the form ax + b = cx + d

Solve.

46. $2x + 2 = x + 8$

(A) 2   (B) -6 (C) $\dfrac{1}{6}$ (D) 6

47. $10x - 8 = x + 17$

(A) $\dfrac{1}{5}$ (B) $\dfrac{9}{25}$ (C) $2\dfrac{7}{9}$ (D) $-2\dfrac{7}{9}$

48. $0.5e - 0.02 = -0.2e + 2.08$

(A) 2.94   (B) -2.94 (C) 3   (D) -3

49. $3 + x = 4x - 3$

(A) -5 (B) 0   (C) 2   (D) -9

50. $-9 - x = 2x + 3$

Objective B: To solve an equation containing parentheses

Solve.

51. $2(x - 1) = 8$

(A) -5 (B) $-\dfrac{9}{2}$ (C) 5   (D) $\dfrac{9}{2}$

Solve.

52. $x + 3 = 2(2x - 3)$

   (A) $\dfrac{7}{3}$　　　　　(B) 2　　　　　(C) -1　　　　　(D) 3

53. $-3 = 7(x - 5) - x$

   (A) $5\dfrac{1}{3}$　　　　(B) $1\dfrac{1}{3}$　　　　(C) $-1\dfrac{1}{3}$　　　　(D) $-5\dfrac{1}{3}$

54. $1 = 5(x - 3) + 5 - 4x$

   (A) 11　　　　　(B) 21　　　　　(C) 9　　　　　(D) -1

55. $(x + 5) + 5 = 2(x - 4) + 1$

Section 11.5: Translating Verbal Expressions into Mathematical Expressions

Objective A: To translate a verbal expression into a mathematical expression given the variable

Translate into a variable expression.

56. 25 pounds less than $\dfrac{1}{3}$ the weight of a shipment of books, where s is the total weight

   (A) $3s - 25$　　　　(B) $\dfrac{s}{3} - 25$　　　　(C) $\dfrac{s - 25}{3}$　　　　(D) $3(s - 25)$

57. the product of n and h

   (A) $n \div h$　　　　(B) $n - h$　　　　(C) $n \cdot h$　　　　(D) $n + h$

58. 7 times the sum of q and 4

   (A) $7(q + 4)$　　　(B) $7 + (q + 4)$　　　(C) $\dfrac{7}{q + 4}$　　　(D) $7 + 4q$

59. five more than z

   (A) $5z$　　　　(B) $z - 5$　　　　(C) $z + 5$　　　　(D) $z \times 5$

Translate into a variable expression.

60. the sum of 3 times m and n

Objective B: To translate a verbal expression into a mathematical expression by assigning the variable

Translate into a variable expression.

61. the quotient of 6 times a number and 11

(A) $\dfrac{6x}{11}$ (B) $\dfrac{6}{11x}$ (C) $\dfrac{11x}{6}$ (D) $\dfrac{11}{6x}$

62. the product of -8 and the sum of 5 times a number and -3

(A) $-8(5x-3)$ (B) $-8 + 5x - 3$ (C) $(x)(-x)(-x)(-x)(-x)-3$ (D) $-8(5x)-3$

63. the difference between a number and sixteen less than the number

(A) $x-(-x-16)$ (B) $x-(x-16)$ (C) $-x-16$ (D) $2x-16$

64. the quotient of nineteen and the sum of a number and twenty

(A) $19x+20$ (B) $\dfrac{19}{x+20}$ (C) $\dfrac{19x}{x+20}$ (D) $19(x+20)$

65. the product of nine-tenths and the difference of a number and eighteen

Section 11.6: Translating Sentences into Equations and Solving

Objective A: To translate a sentence into an equation and solve

Translate into an equation and solve.

66. The sum of five times a number and thirteen is twenty-eight. Find the number.

(A) $5x+13=28$; 3 (B) $5x+28=13$; -3 (C) $28x\times5=13$; 2 (D) $x+65=28$; -37

67. The difference between twelve and a number is one. Find the number.

(A) $1=x-12$; 11 (B) $1-x=12$; 11 (C) $12-x=1$; 11 (D) $x-12=1$; 11

Translate into an equation and solve.

68. The quotient of twenty and a number is four. Find the number.

(A) $\dfrac{20}{x}=20;\ 4$ (B) $\dfrac{20}{x}=4;\ 5$ (C) $\dfrac{x}{20}=4;\ 5$ (D) $\dfrac{x}{20}=4;\ 4$

69. The product of three and a number is negative thirty. Find the number.

(A) $\dfrac{x}{3}=-30;\ 3$ (B) $x+3=-30;\ 3$ (C) $3x=-30;\ -10$ (D) $x-3=-30;\ -10$

70. Five times the sum of twice a number and five is thirty-five. Find the number.

Objective B: To solve application problems

71. Starlight Tree Farm sells Douglas firs and noble firs. One December they sold 183 more Douglas firs than noble firs. The total number of trees sold was 473. Which equation could be used to solve for n, the number of noble fir trees sold?

(A) $n+183=473$ (B) $n-183=473$ (C) $2n+183=473$ (D) $2n-183=473$

72. Takima has 14 more coins than Mei-Lin. Takima has 43 coins. Which equation could be solved to find how many coins Mei-Lin has?

(A) $x+43=-14$ (B) $x-14=43$ (C) $x+43=14$ (D) $x+14=43$

73. Sam is 18 years old, which is 15 less than 3 times Mickey's age. Which equation could be used to solve for Mickey's age? How old is Mickey?

(A) $15x-3=18;\ 1\text{ yr}$ (B) $3x-15=18;\ 11\text{ yr}$
(C) $3x+15=18;\ 1\text{ yr}$ (D) $15x-3=18;\ 1.4\text{ yr}$

74. Andrew has 12 more gloves than Lee. Andrew has 35 gloves. Which equation can be used to find how many gloves Lee has? How many gloves does Lee have?

(A) $x+12=35;\ 23$ (B) $x-12=35;\ 47$ (C) $x\le 12;\ 35$ (D) $x\ge 12;\ 35$

75. The science club is selling puzzles to raise money. The supplier charges a one-time fee of $80 for each order and $2 for each puzzle. Write and solve an equation for the number of puzzles the science club can purchase if their budget is $500.

Chapter 11 Introduction to Algebra

Section 11.1: Variable Expressions

Objective A: To evaluate variable expressions

[1] (D)

[2] (B)

[3] (B)

[4] (B)

[5] 0.1

Objective B: To simplify variable expressions containing no parenthesis

[6] (D)

[7] (B)

[8] (C)

[9] (A)

[10] $-5x^4 - 2x^2$

Objective C: To simplify variable expressions containing parentheses

[11] (B)

[12] (D)

[13] (D)

[14] (B)

[15] $x - 8$ _____

Section 11.2: Introduction to Equations

Objective A: To determine whether a given value is a solution of an equation

[16] (D) _____

[17] (D) _____

[18] (C) _____

[19] (A) _____

[20] Yes _____

Objective B: To solve an equation of the form x + a = b

[21] (D) _____

[22] (B) _____

[23] (B) _____

[24] (B) _____

[25] 12 _____

Objective C: To solve an equation of the form ax = b

[26] (C) _____

[27] (D) _____

[28] (C) _____

[29] (A) _____

[30] $\dfrac{23}{3}$ _____

Objective D: To solve application problems

[31] (D) _____

[32] (A) _____

[33] (B) _____

[34] (D) _____

[35] 412 _____

Section 11.3: General Equations: Part 1

Objective A: To solve an equation of the form ax + b = c

[36] (A) _____

[37] (A) _____

[38] (A) _____

[39] (C) _____

[40] −2 _____

Objective B: To solve application problems

[41] (D) _____

[42] (D) _____

[43] (B) _____

[44] (B) _____

[45] 14 pennies and 42 nickels _____

Section 11.4: General Equations: Part 2

Objective A: To solve an equation of the form $ax + b = cx + d$

[46] (D) _____

[47] (C) _____

[48] (C) _____

[49] (C) _____

[50] -4 _____

Objective B: To solve an equation containing parentheses

[51] (C) _____

[52] (D) _____

[53] (A) _____

[54] (A) _____

[55] 17 _____

Section 11.5: Translating Verbal Expressions into Mathematical Expressions

Objective A: To translate a verbal expression into a mathematical expression given the variable

[56] (B) ____

[57] (C) ____

[58] (A) ____

[59] (C) ____

[60] $3m+n$ ____

Objective B: To translate a verbal expression into a mathematical expression by assigning the variable

[61] (A) ____

[62] (A) ____

[63] (B) ____

[64] (B) ____

[65] $\frac{9}{10}(x-18)$ or $\frac{9}{10}x-\frac{81}{5}$ ____

Section 11.6: Translating Sentences into Equations and Solving

Objective A: To translate a sentence into an equation and solve

[66] (A) ____

[67] (C) ____

[68] (B) ____

[69] (C)

[70] $5(2x+5)=35;\ 1$

Objective B: To solve application problems

[71] (C)

[72] (D)

[73] (B)

[74] (A)

[75] $2n+80=500;\ 210$ puzzles

Section 12.1: Angles, Lines, and Geometric Figures

Objective A: To define and describe lines and angles

1. Which statement is true according to the diagram?

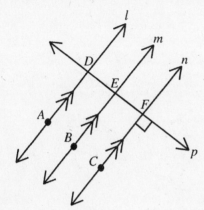

   (A) $\overleftrightarrow{AD} \perp \overleftrightarrow{DF}$ (B) $\overleftrightarrow{BE} \perp \overleftrightarrow{CF}$ (C) $\overleftrightarrow{AD} \parallel \overleftrightarrow{DF}$ (D) $\overleftrightarrow{BE} \parallel \overleftrightarrow{DF}$

2. Which is the best description of perpendicular line segments?

   (A) lines that do not intersect   (B) line segments that intersect to form a right angle

   (C) lines that intersect to form a right angle   (D) line segments that do not intersect

3. Choose the symbol notation and name for the geometric figure.

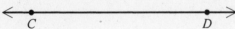

   (A) $\overline{CD}$; segment   (B) $\overrightarrow{CD}$; ray   (C) $\overleftrightarrow{CD}$; line   (D) $\overrightarrow{DC}$; ray

4. If $AB = 17$ and $BC = 11$, find AC.

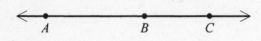

   (A) 29   (B) 27   (C) 56   (D) 28

5. Name all angles having *M* as their vertex.

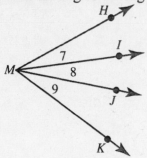

Objective B: To define and describe geometric figures

6. Find the measure of the missing angle.

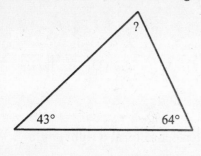

(A) 253   (B) 73   (C) 287   (D) 107

7. Which is the measure of angle x?

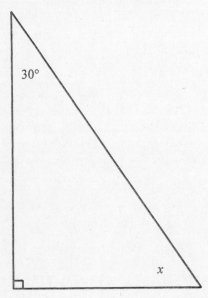

(A) 60   (B) 150   (C) 28   (D) 30

8. In triangle ABC, $m\angle A = 59$ and $m\angle C = 30$. Calculate $m\angle B$.

(A) 101   (B) 1   (C) 87   (D) 91

9. The radius of a circle is 10 centimeters. Which is its diameter?

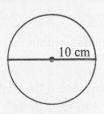

(A) 30 cm   (B) 20 cm   (C) 40 cm   (D) 5 cm

10. What is the most general name of the quadrilateral that is defined as having exactly one pair of parallel sides?

Objective C: To solve problems involving angles formed by intersecting lines

11. Given that $\overleftrightarrow{PQ}$ and $\overleftrightarrow{RS}$ are parallel, find $m\angle 1$.

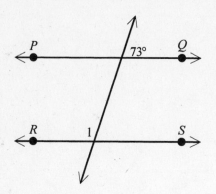

    (A) 117°   (B) 73°   (C) 107°   (D) 17°

12. In the figure shown, $m\angle AED = 121$. Which of the following statements is false?

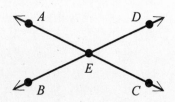

    (A) $\angle AEB$ and $\angle DEC$ are vertical angles   (B) $m\angle BEC = 59$

    (C) $m\angle AEB = 59$ (D) $\angle BEC$ and $\angle CED$ are adjacent angles

13. In order to set up for a fair, Janis divides the field into four sections by putting out two lines of rope that intersect in the middle of the the field. The regions are numbered from one to four in a clockwise manner. If the angle at the point of intersection for region 3 has a magnitude of 86°, which is the measure of the angle of region 2?

    (A) 86   (B) 94   (C) 47   (D) 172

14. Which is the measure of $\angle POQ$?

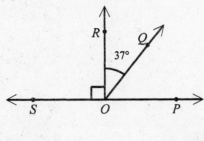

    (A) 90°   (B) 37°   (C) 53°   (D) none of these

15. In the figure shown, $m\angle AED = 131$.

True or False: $\angle AEB$ and $\angle AED$ are supplementary and $m\angle AEB = 49$.

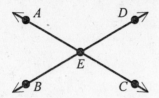

Section 12.2: Plane Geometric Figures

Objective A: To find the perimeter of plane geometric figures

16. Calculate the circumference of the circle. Use $3.14 = \pi$.

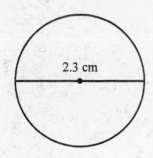

2.3 cm

    (A) 7.222 cm   (B) 3.611 cm   (C) 4.153 cm   (D) 5.44 cm

17. Which is the perimeter of the triangle?

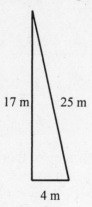

17 m 25 m

4 m

(A) 46 m (B) 138 m (C) 92 m (D) 1700 m

18. Find the perimeter of the rectangle.

5 ft

9 ft

(A) 45 ft (B) 14 ft (C) 28 ft (D) 30 ft

19. Find the perimeter of a square with sides that are $17\frac{1}{8}$ inches long.

(A) $68\frac{1}{2}$ in. (B) $293\frac{17}{64}$ in. (C) $55\frac{21}{32}$ in. (D) $34\frac{1}{4}$ in.

20. Find the perimeter of a rectangle that is 40 by 37 yards.

Objective B: To find the perimeter of composite geometric figures

21. Find the perimeter of this figure. Dimensions are in feet. All angles are right angles.

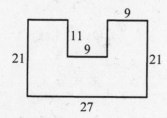

9

11
9

21 21

27

(A) 118 ft (B) 96 ft (C) 59 ft (D) 129 ft

22. Which is the perimeter of this figure? Dimensions are in centimeters. Use 3.14 for π.

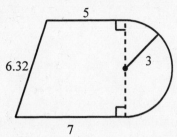

(A) 27.74 cm   (B) 33.74 cm   (C) 37.16 cm   (D) 24.32 cm

23. Bob is fencing the area shown below.

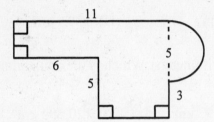

If all measurements are given in feet, how many feet of fence will he need?

(A) $33+5\pi$ (B) $33+\dfrac{25}{4}\pi$ (C) $33+\dfrac{5}{2}\pi$ (D) $33+3\pi$

24. Find the perimeter of the figure. All angles that appear to be right angles are right angles. Dimensions are in centimeters.

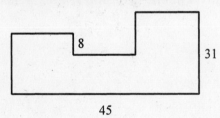

(A) 252 cm   (B) 78 cm   (C) 158 cm   (D) 168 cm

25. Find the perimeter of the figure.

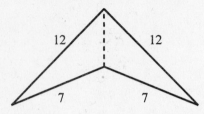

Objective C: To solve application problems

26. The diamond-shaped windows in a railroad dining car need to have metal frames made for them. Each edge of a window measures 45.1 centimeters. How much metal is needed to make the frame for one window?

(A) 180.4 cm   (B) 135.3 cm   (C) 182 cm   (D) 138.9 cm

27. The distance around the equator of Saturn is about 378,675 kilometers. Which is the equatorial diameter of Saturn? Use $3.14 = \pi$.

(A) 241,209 km   (B) 241,194 km   (C) 120,597 km   (D) 120,584 km

28. A wooden fence is to be built around a 34- by 40-meter lot. How many meters of fencing will be needed? If the wood for the fence costs $44.50 per meter, what will the wood for the fence cost?

(A) 148 m; $6586.00   (B) 148 m; $60,520.00

(C) 1360 m; $60,520.00   (D) 1360 m; $6586.00

29. How far does the horse on the edge of the merry-go-round travel in one revolution? The radius of the merry-go-round is 24 feet. Use 3.14 for π.

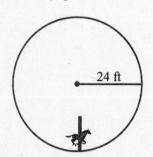

(A) 75.36 ft   (B) 150.72 ft   (C) 37.68 ft   (D) 1808.64 ft

30. Christine ran 3 times around a circular track that has a radius of 41 meters. Write the best approximation of the distance she ran. Use $3.14 = \pi$.

Section 12.3: Area

Objective A: To find the area of geometric figures

31. Find the area of the rectangle.

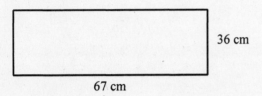

                 36 cm

     67 cm

(A) 1206 cm^2 (B) 206 cm^2 (C) 2412 cm^2 (D) 103 cm^2

32. Find the area.

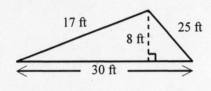

(A) 255 ft^2 (B) 120 ft^2 (C) 33 ft^2 (D) 200 ft^2

33. Find the area of the circle. Use $3.14 = \pi$..

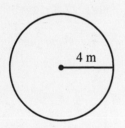

(A) 50.24 m^2 (B) 200.96 m^2 (C) 25.12 m^2 (D) 12.56 m^2

34. Find the area of a square with a side of length 21.8 millimeters.

(A) 950.48 mm^2 (B) 87.2 mm^2 (C) 475.24 mm^2 (D) 43.6 mm^2

35. Find the area of a triangular piece of cloth with a 6-centimeter base and 20-centimeter height.

Objective B: To find the area of composite geometric figures

36. Find the area of the shaded region. Use $3.14 = \pi$.

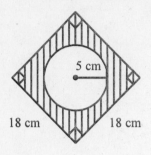

(A) 78.54 cm²   (B) 169 cm²   (C) 245.46 cm²   (D) 292.58 cm²

37. Find the area of the figure. Dimensions are in centimeters. Use $3.14 = \pi$.

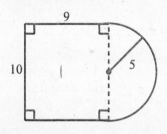

(A) 78.5 cm²   (B) 168.5 cm²   (C) 129.25 cm²   (D) 97.85 cm²

38. Find the area of the region shown.

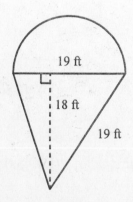

(A) $(180.5\pi + 171)$ ft²   (B) $(361\pi + 180.5)$ ft²

(C) $(45.125\pi + 171)$ ft²   (D) $(28.5\pi + 28)$ ft²

39. Find the area of the region shown.

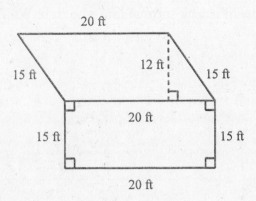

(A) 100 ft^2 (B) 480 ft^2 (C) 600 ft^2 (D) 540 ft^2

40. Find the area of this figure. Dimensions are in feet.

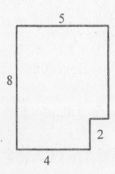

Objective C: To solve application problems

41. The figure below represents the overhead view of a deck surrounding a hot tub. Which is the area of the deck? Use $3.14 = \pi$.

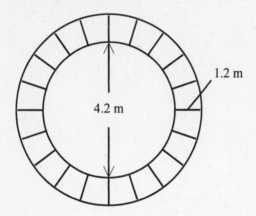

1.2 m

4.2 m

    (A) 34.2 m²   (B) 20.3 m²   (C) 13.8 m²   (D) 122.9 m²

42. A piece of fabric measures 35 by 44 inches. A triangular scarf with a height of 25 inches and a base of 30 inches is cut from the fabric. How much fabric is left over?

    (A) 582.5 in²   (B) 1165 in²   (C) 395 in²   (D) 790 in²

43. Find the cost of carpet for an office that measures 21 feet by 24 feet if the carpet costs $16.50 per square yard.

    (A) $1386.00   (B) $2772.00   (C) $8316.00   (D) $924.00

44. The rectangular part of the field below is 140 yards long, and the diameter of each semicircle is 42 yards. Find the cost of fertilizing the field at $0.10 per square yard.

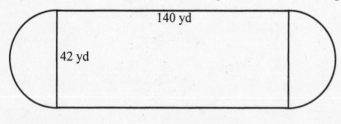

140 yd

42 yd

    (A) $657.27   (B) $726.54   (C) $432.54   (D) $1142.18

45. A lot measures 36 by 31 meters. A swimming pool, 7 by 5 meters, is placed on the lot. How much area is left over?

Section 12.4: Volume

Objective A: To find the volume of geometric solids

46. Find the volume of the sphere. Use $3.14 = \pi$.

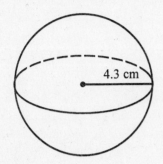

4.3 cm

(A) 333 cm^3 (B) 187 cm^3 (C) 346 cm^3 (D) 77 cm^3

47. Find the volume of the cylinder. Use $3.14 = \pi$.

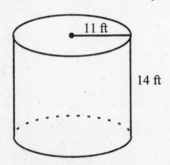

11 ft

14 ft

(A) 483.56 ft^3 (B) 1694 ft^3 (C) 6769.84 ft^3 (D) 5319.16 ft^3

48. Find the volume of the rectangle.

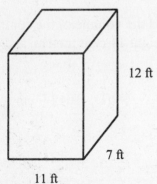

12 ft

7 ft

11 ft

(A) 924 ft^3 (B) 120 ft^3 (C) 944 ft^3 (D) 586 ft^3

49. Find the volume of a rectangular prism that is 5 centimeters long, 2 centimeters wide, and 7 centimeters high.

(A) 14 cm^3 (B) 70 cm^3 (C) 118 cm^3 (D) none of these

50. Find the volume.

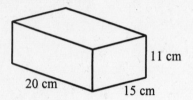

Objective B: To find the volume of composite geometric solids

51. Find the volume. Use 3.14 for π.

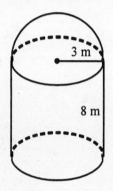

(A) 244.92 m^3 (B) 339.12 m^3 (C) 282.6 m^3 (D) 128.52 m^3

52. A rectangular pyramid fits exactly on top of a rectangular prism. Find the volume of the composite figure if the prism has length 17 centimeters, width 4 centimeters, height 11 centimeters, and the pyramid has height 13 centimeters.

(A) 748 cm^3 (B) $294\frac{2}{3}$ cm^3 (C) 1632 cm^3 (D) $1042\frac{2}{3}$ cm^3

53. Estimate the volume of the composite figure.

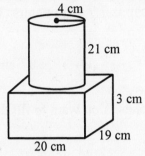

(A) 30 cm^3 (B) 2160 cm^3 (C) 400 cm^3 (D) 220 cm^3

54. Find the volume of the composite figure.

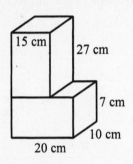

(A) 5486 cm^3 (B) 6800 cm^3 (C) 5450 cm^3 (D) 2170 cm^3

55. Calculate, to the nearest tenth, the remaining volume of metal in a 12.2-centimeter metal cube after a hole 8 centimeters in diameter is drilled through it perpendicular to a face. Use $3.14 = \pi$.

Objective C: To solve application problems

56. A satellite is made of a cylinder and two hemispheres that fit snugly on either end. If the diameter of the cylinder is 18 meters, and the length is 18 meters, find the volume of the satellite in terms of π.

(A) 13,608π m^3 (B) 1566π m^3 (C) 2430π m^3 (D) 594π m^3

57. A canister, 15 centimeters high and 15.5 centimeters in diameter, is filled with flour 2 centimeters from the top. Which volume of flour, to the nearest cubic centimeter, does the canister contain?

(A) 2452 cm^3 (B) 377 cm^3 (C) 2384 cm^3 (D) 2829 cm^3

58. A thermos is in the shape of a cylinder with a hemispherical cap. The height of the whole thermos (both cylinder and cap) is 21 centimeters, while the diameter of the cap is 7.7 centimeters. Which is the volume of the thermos, including the cap? Use $3.14 = \pi$.

    (A) 917.67 cm³   (B) 1096.86 cm³   (C) 1574.69 cm³   (D) 1933.07 cm³

59. A fish tank is 23 inches tall and has a base that is 17 inches by 24 inches. You want to fill the tank to a depth of 21 inches. How much water will it take?

    (A) 9384 in³   (B) 2538 in³   (C) 8686 in³   (D) 8568 in³

60. Three balls are packaged in a cylindrical container as shown below. If the balls just touch the top, bottom, and sides of the cylinder, and the diameter of a single ball is 6 centimeters, how much of the space inside the cylinder is not filled by the balls? Use $3.14 = \pi$ and round your answer to the nearest cubic centimeter.

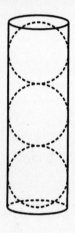

Section 12.5: The Pythagorean Theorem

Objective A: To find the square root of a number

61. Calculate $\sqrt{8}$ to the nearest thousandth.

    (A) 2.830   (B) 2.828   (C) 2.829   (D) 2.827

62. Which two whole numbers are closest to $\sqrt{159}$?

    (A) 12 and 13   (B) 158 and 160   (C) 11 and 12   (D) 13 and 14

63. $\sqrt{169} = $ ___

    (A) 130   (B) 1.3   (C) 13   (D) 169

64. Evaluate. $\sqrt{36} + \sqrt{144} + \sqrt{16} + \sqrt{169}$

    (A) $\sqrt{35}$ (B) 365   (C) $\sqrt{365}$ (D) 35

65. Find the number which has a square root of 9.

Objective B: To find the unknown side of a right triangle using the Pythagorean Theorem

66. Find x.

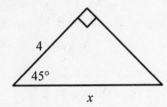

    (A) 6.928   (B) 5.657   (C) 11.314   (D) 8.000

67. Given the right triangle below, what is the length of the hypotenuse?

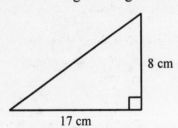

    (A) $\sqrt{363}$ cm   (B) $\sqrt{353}$ cm   (C) 353 cm   (D) 15 cm

68. Find the perimeter of the triangle.

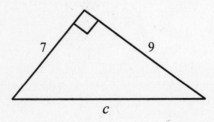

    (A) 32.0   (B) 27.4   (C) 22.8   (D) 11.4

69. $\triangle ABC$ is a right triangle with hypotenuse c and legs of length a and b. If $a = 15$ and $c = 17$, then $b =$ ___.

(A) 32   (B) 16   (C) 2   (D) 8

70. Find x.

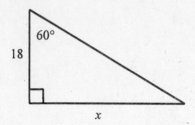

Objective C: To solve application problems

71. Mr. Jones built a fenced-in area for his horse in the shape of a square with each side 40 feet in length. Find the distance of the diagonal path from one corner to the opposite corner.

(A) 160.000 ft   (B) 1600.000 ft   (C) 3200.000 ft   (D) 56.569 ft

72. A telephone pole breaks and falls as shown.

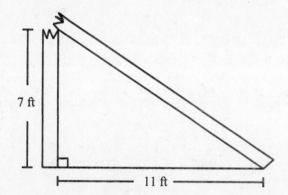

To the nearest foot, what was the original height of the pole?

(A) 20 ft   (B) 19 ft   (C) 21 ft   (D) 22 ft

73. The city commission wants to construct a new street that connects Main Street and North Boulevard as shown in the diagram below. The construction cost has been estimated at $100 per linear foot. Find the estimated cost for building the street.

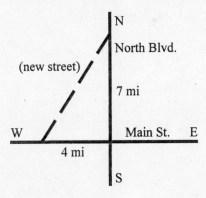

    (A) $4,256,872   (B) $42,569   (C) $806   (D) $528,000

74. Wayne used the diagram to compute the distance from Ferris to Dunlap to Butte. How much shorter is the distance directly from Ferris to Butte than the distance Wayne found?

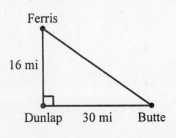

    (A) 46 mi   (B) 34 mi   (C) 12 mi   (D) 20 mi

75. A boat in calm seas travels in a straight line and ends the trip 31 kilometers west and 41 kilometers north of its original position. Find the distance of the trip to the nearest tenth of a kilometer.

Section 12.6: Simpliar and Congruent Triangles

Objective A: To solve similar and congruent triangles

76. The two triangles are congruent. Find the missing side lengths and angle measures.

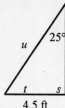 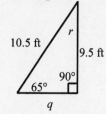

(A) $q = 4.5$ ft; $r = 25°$; $s = 65°$; $t = 90°$; $u = 4.5$ ft

(B) $q = 9.5$ ft; $r = 25°$; $s = 90°$; $t = 65°$; $u = 10.5$ ft

(C) $q = 4.5$ ft; $r = 25°$; $s = 90°$; $t = 65°$; $u = 4.5$ ft

(D) $q = 4.5$ ft; $r = 25°$; $s = 90°$; $t = 65°$; $u = 10.5$ ft

77. Use similar triangles to find x.

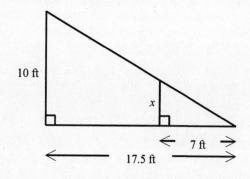

(A) 25 ft   (B) 12.25 ft   (C) 4 ft   (D) 0.97 ft

78. Triangles ABC and DEF are similar. Find x and y.

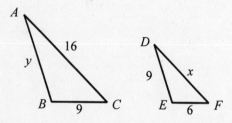

(A) $x = 10.67$, $y = 12.5$ (B) $x = 10.67$, $y = 13.5$

(C) $x = 11.67$, $y = 13.5$ (D) $x = 11.67$, $y = 12.5$

79. Triangles *DHE* and *RPS* are similar. Which proportion correctly identifies the corresponding sides?

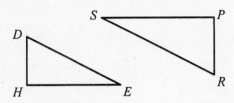

(A) $\dfrac{DH}{RS} = \dfrac{DE}{RP} = \dfrac{HE}{RS}$

(B) $\dfrac{DH}{PS} = \dfrac{DE}{RP} = \dfrac{HE}{RS}$

(C) $\dfrac{DH}{RP} = \dfrac{DE}{RS} = \dfrac{HE}{PS}$

(D) $\dfrac{DH}{HD} = \dfrac{RP}{SR} = \dfrac{HE}{EH}$

80. $\triangle DEF$ and $\triangle GHI$ are similar. If *DE*, *EF*, *DF*, and *GH* are 6 inches, 8 inches, 9 inches, and 7.4 inches respectively, find *GI* to the nearest tenth.

Objective B: To solve application problems

81. The extendable ramp shown below is used to move crates of fruit to loading docks of different heights. When the horizontal distance *AB* is 6 feet, the height of the loading dock, *BC*, is 3 feet. Which is the height of the loading dock, *DE*?

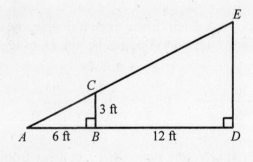

(A) 108 ft   (B) 18 ft   (C) 9 ft   (D) 6 ft

82. Two ladders are leaning against a wall at the same angle as shown.

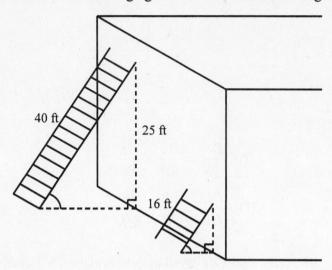

How far up the wall does the shorter ladder reach?

(A) 14 ft   (B) 10 ft   (C) 20 ft   (D) 8 ft

83. Standing next to each other, a man who is 67 inches tall casts a 80.4-inch shadow and his son casts a 45.6-inch shadow. What is the height of the son to the nearest inch?

(A) 36   (B) 118   (C) 55   (D) 38

84. A lamppost is 27 feet high and casts a 36-foot shadow at noon. At the same time, a flagpole next to the lamppost casts a 48-foot shadow. Which proportion can be used to find the height, *H*, of the flagpole?

(A) $\dfrac{H}{48} = \dfrac{27}{36}$ (B) $\dfrac{H}{48} = \dfrac{36}{27}$ (C) $\dfrac{36}{48} = \dfrac{H}{27}$ (D) $\dfrac{H}{36} = \dfrac{27}{48}$

85. Mandy wants to find the height of the tallest building in her city. She stands 461 feet away from the building. There is a tree 34 feet in front of her, which she knows is 17 feet tall. How tall is the building? Round to the nearest foot.

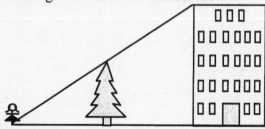

Chapter 12 Geometry

Section 12.1: Angles, Lines, and Geometric Figures

Objective A: To define and describe lines and angles

[1] (A)

[2] (B)

[3] (C)

[4] (D)

[5] ∠7, ∠8, ∠9, ∠HMJ, ∠IMK, ∠HMK

Objective B: To define and describe geometric figures

[6] (B)

[7] (A)

[8] (D)

[9] (B)

[10] trapezoid

Objective C: To solve problems involving angles formed by intersecting lines

[11] (C)

[12] (B)

[13] (B)

[14] (C)

[15] True

Section 12.2: Plane Geometric Figures

Objective A: To find the perimeter of plane geometric figures

[16] (A)

[17] (A)

[18] (C)

[19] (A)

[20] 154 yd

Objective B: To find the perimeter of composite geometric figures

[21] (A)

[22] (A)

[23] (C)

[24] (D)

[25] 38

Objective C: To solve application problems

[26] (A)

[27] (C)

[28] (A)

[29] (B)

[30] 772.44 m

Section 12.3: Area

Objective A: To find the area of geometric figures

[31] (C)

[32] (B)

[33] (A)

[34] (C)

[35] 60 cm^2

Objective B: To find the area of composite geometric figures

[36] (C)

[37] (C)

[38] (C)

[39] (D)

[40] 38 ft^2

Objective C: To solve application problems

[41] (B)

[42] (B)

[43] (D)

[44] (B)

[45] 1081 m^2

Section 12.4: Volume

Objective A: To find the volume of geometric solids

[46] (A)

[47] (D)

[48] (A)

[49] (B)

[50] 3300 cm^3

Objective B: To find the volume of composite geometric solids

[51] (C)

[52] (D)

[53] (B)

[54] (C)

[55] 1202.9 cm^3

Objective C: To solve application problems

[56] (C)

[57] (A) _____

[58] (A) _____

[59] (D) _____

[60] 170 cm³ _____

Section 12.5: The Pythagorean Theorem

Objective A: To find the square root of a number

[61] (B) _____

[62] (A) _____

[63] (C) _____

[64] (D) _____

[65] 81 _____

Objective B: To find the unknown side of a right triangle using the Pythagorean Theorem

[66] (B) _____

[67] (B) _____

[68] (B) _____

[69] (D) _____

[70] $18\sqrt{3}$ _____

Objective C: To solve application problems

[71] (D)

[72] (A)

[73] (A)

[74] (C)

[75] 51.4 km

Section 12.6: Simpliar and Congruent Triangles

Objective A: To solve similar and congruent triangles

[76] (D)

[77] (C)

[78] (B)

[79] (C)

[80] 11.1 in.

Objective B: To solve application problems

[81] (C)

[82] (B)

[83] (D)

[84] (A)

[85] 231 ft _____